# THE MYSTICAL HEXAGRAM:

## The Seven Inner Stars of Power

G. Michael Vasey

&

Sue Vincent

ISBN: - 0996197214

ISBN 13: - 978-0-9961972-1-2

Now also available as an online course from Brno Earth Magic school on Teachable - https://earth-magic-brno.teachable.com/ for more information and to sign up!

# Table of Contents

# Saturn and Lead

*Of Saturn and Lead I speak*
*The basest metal of all*
*Heaviness, darkness*
*Hidden from the light*
*My soul sees the night*

*A burden I cannot carry*
*Instincts abandoned return*
*Spiralling downward*
*Galena's sulfur suffocates*
*All that Saturn advocates*

*Saturnalia is explained*
*Deep need for some relief*
*Base needs expunged*
*A temporary respite*
*Daytime during night*

*Daath sees from on high*
*These things I must leave behind*
*My throat begs to speak*
*Words chosen with care*
*My soul now laid bare*

*As Emperor I see*
*Father to my imaginings*
*Mother to my world*
*Saturn's child consumed*
*Now- my life resumes*

# Preface to the first edition

The main thesis and content of this book arose out of meditation and reflection over several years following completion of the Servants of the Light (SOL) first degree course (Butler version). So far as I know it is original content although as the meditations developed, I began to see the validity of what was coming through all over the place. Readers of the book "Inner Journeys: Explorations of the Soul" will know that the beginnings of this communication began with the discovery of an inner contact – Asteroth – but they have continued until this day. In many respects, this work is incomplete. It will always be incomplete as the revelations of continuing meditations and communication with contacts continues to cast more and more light on these matters.

At some point, however, one must pass on what has been learned. Indeed, I was told that this is something that I should do. What is written here is what it is. I have faith and believe that those who are inclined to understand it will have some use for it. Despite that, it is imperfect and unfinished, and will in all honesty always be that way for it is simply an ego-tainted glimpse of some much more significant truth beyond my understanding.

The reader will also find very few references to other authors in the main part of this book and that is deliberate. Early in the meditation work I was inclined to seek verification and support else-where but frankly, I soon discovered that this simply was somehow distracting. I therefore decided to rely on my inner thoughts and only supplement them, if necessary, with external reference material.

This book may never have been written at all except for the cajoling of certain individuals including Dolores Ashcroft-Nowicki (Director of Studies, Servants of the Light), to whom I will be eternally indebted for showing me kindness and always stretching me to goals that I didn't believe I could achieve. Indeed, many SOLers have helped one way or another in both my personal development as well in helping get this book written. But the biggest thanks go to my co-author – Sue Vincent.

Sue, at the time of writing and publication, I had never met in person, began corresponding with me some years ago after visiting my blog. I discovered in Sue a person filled with radiant light that always assisted and helped those around here unselfishly without significant thought for herself. She was also a talented artist. She also encouraged me to get this book out and in so doing rose to the challenge to help me by editing, writing certain chapters and creating all the artwork. I thank her profusely.

Finally, if this work is an error or contains error then I alone take personal responsibility for that. I am confident that what is written here was received from reliable sources and only my ego-centered self can be responsible for any error or misunderstanding.

G. Michael Vasey

*Prague, Czech Republic.*

*2012*

# Preface to the Second Edition

A second edition so soon?

Yes, because this is a work in progress and possibly always will be. There were changes and additions we wished to make and so a new version was needed. These have been made. We have also tidied it up a little removing several short and possibly superfluous short articles at the front of the book. We think the result is a more readable work.

Since the book was first published, much has changed. While one of us continues to be somewhat of a solo practitioner and affiliated as a second degree initiate and supervisor with the Servants of the Light (SOL), the other has co-founded an entirely new school of consciousness, The Silent Eye, which seeks to bring an awareness of the magic of life into the everyday world. ...Meanwhile, G. Michael Vasey pursues Bardon's approach via his book *Initiation into Hermetics* as he tries to master the elements and himself.

Both of us are readily contactable and interested to hear of your experiences with use of the exercises in this book and insights into the Hexagram.

In Light,

G. Michael Vasey                    Sue Vincent

*Czech Republic*                    *England. May 2015*

# Foreword

It is with pleasure that I introduce this book to our SOL students and seekers of knowledge. All too often a newcomer to occult training is left to flounder their way through terms and symbols with no proper explanation of their meaning or origin.

Gary Vasey and Sue Vincent have done a great service in taking some of the most common and yet unexplained symbols and set themselves the task of making them familiar and understandable. At my age I am constantly amazed at the books now on offer to students. I think back to my own days of training when, if it was not fully explained by your teacher, you were left to puzzle it out by yourself. To have books like this close to hand and written with clarity and attention to detail by someone fully conversant with the subject is nothing short of a marvel to me.

I was lucky enough to have a teacher with patience to spare, many do not, so this book comes to the rescue with a precise explanation of everything you need to know. Written by two people who have the knowledge at their fingertips and the experience to back it up it is more than worthy of a place on your bookshelves. I highly recommend it to all our SOL students, and it will be added to the required reading list for SOL training.

Dolores Ashcroft-Nowicki

*Director of Studies SOL*

# Associations of the Hexagram

A symbol is a representation of a quality or concept. Mankind has always used symbols to share ideas. Language is a series of symbols, used in infinite combination, to communicate complex ideas. From the earliest times, our species has used visual symbols to convey information, share abstract ideas and consolidate knowledge. Cave paintings such as those from the Lascaux caverns in France still move us with tales of the hunt some 30,000 years after they were created, providing a window through time to show us the grace and beauty of the world of our ancestors.

In this book, we explore a single, geometric shape - the hexagram. Throughout history this shape has appeared spontaneously in many cultures and has many variants on meaning and interpretation. At least on the surface. However, the more one looks at any symbol, the deeper one delves, the more apparent it becomes that symbols have a universal appeal and speak to us at a level which transcends the artificial barriers of culture, reaching into the viscera of humankind.

The esoteric theory behind this universal understanding may perhaps best be illustrated by a single symbol that has permeated global mythology: the sun. Our far ancestors looked at the sky and saw a great golden globe. It gave warmth and light, which meant safety, food, and comfort. Like a watchful eye, it rode the heavens each day and disappeared beyond the horizon at night. In the hours of darkness life was cold and dangerous. Dawn brought the sun's return and the renewal of life. Winter saw the sun retreat, weakened and cold. Food was scarce, life was fragile and the hours of darkness long.

It takes little imagination to understand how our distant fathers learned to equate the sun with life, health, and protection. Ancient solar symbols testify to their worship of the sun and their instinctive understanding of its life-giving virtue. One can imagine how, as communities evolved, sharing the captured gift of sunlight reflected in the Hearth fire, stories were woven to illustrate the power of this heavenly orb. Mythologies grew and were intertwined with faith and hope, becoming religions.

Supplication and propitiation, worship, and prayer... all would have been offered to the Sun god. The more concentrated the worship, the more the symbol of the Sun would have assumed a powerful place in the mind of Man. Abstract thought allowed the symbolism to be connected to other ideas, and the light which kept the beasts at bay became the Light towards which Mankind has always turned.

On the subtler levels, the continuous concentration of awe, worship and prayer consolidated the images we had created to symbolise the power of the visible sun. By focusing on these symbols of Light, we tap into both the Form of the human vision that was built to encapsulate a series of abstract ideas, and the very real and universal Force that symbol was designed to represent.

Symbols mean nothing by themselves… they are simply pictures, images. However, by accessing the correspondences, myths, legends, and beliefs with which they are associated we can begin to understand the forces, natural and divine, material, and abstract, which they were designed to represent.

In Ice Age Britain, man carved geometric designs into the walls of caves. We cannot know what they were intended to convey, but we can surmise that our forefathers would not have gone to so much effort without reason! The carvings at Creswell Crags include birds, ibex and bison and were, perhaps, part of an attempt to ensure survival through sympathetic magic. We cannot know why the geometric shapes were included, or what they meant to the man who carved them, but we can appreciate that they had meaning and importance to him.

Geometrical shapes permeate the art and symbolism of all cultures. Some 5,000 years ago, long before Euclid wrote 'The Elements' in the great, lost Library of Alexandria, geometry was being used for practical purposes to solve everyday problems. Geometry demands the capability to think and to visualise in abstract terms, translating a concept into a two-dimensional representation. Art also demands the intellectual freedom to translate ideas and experience into symbols. Yet 70,000 years ago, in Blombos Cave in what is now South Africa, triangles and diamond shapes were being carved into a piece of ochre.

Some scientists have called this the earliest example of abstract art while others dismiss it as mere doodling. Either hypothesis may be true. Perhaps there was meaning to the pattern as it was deliberately cut into the stone, perhaps the mind of the carver flew free into daydream as his hands moved blindly. Perhaps, too, it was simply an expression of beauty. Whatever the interpretation, it serves to illustrate the fact that visual geometry is deeply rooted in the mind of Man.

The hexagram is a symbol that pervades the pages of history and culture. There can be few symbols that have a place at the heart of so many faiths, yet the origins of the hexagram are shrouded in the mists of time.

Today the hexagram is featured on the national flag of Israel and is the symbol of the Zionist Christian Church. Rastafarians use a black hexagram to identify the black population with the tribes of Israel; most branches of Christianity use the Star in architecture and religious art. In Islam, where the prophets and kings of Israel are honoured and revered, the hexagram is also a common architectural motif.

Other Eastern faiths have also used the hexagram. It is essentially a simple shape and, like the other basic geometrical shapes, would have evolved separately in cultures far apart. Curiously, the symbolism implied by its usage remains fundamentally similar, echoing the theme of the masculine, dynamic Blade of the upward pointing triangle embracing in perfect harmony the downward pointing triangle of the feminine, receptive Chalice. This symbolism will, of course, be immediately obvious to those cognisant with the rituals of modern witchcraft.

The mandala called *satkona yantra* is found on many South Indian Hindu Temples, thousands of years old. The shape is generally portrayed as two interlocking triangles, signifying the duality of Man, poised between Heaven and Earth. The downward pointing triangle symbolises Shakti, the divine feminine, the receptive latency of Creation, while the upward pointing triangle represents Shiva, the potent, dynamic, masculine Force. Together they represent the Divine Union. In the mythology, the son that is born of this union is Sanmuga, which means 'the one with six faces.'

In Tibetan, the symbol is called 'chos-kyi 'byung-gnas', the Origin of Phenomenon. Regarded in this light, we again see the fusion of opposites producing a 'child'. Dr. Vasey was advised to '*reconcile the opposites*' and this phrase leads directly to the principles of Alchemy.

Carl Jung realised that the mediaeval Alchemist was working on the transformation of their own psyche, and the 'gold' they were seeking was their own higher self. By 'reconciling the opposites' of, for example, passive and dynamic, divine, and material, and finding the relationship between them, mirrored endlessly within each other, the alchemist was able to achieve a point of perfect balance, poised between the extremes and harmonizing them within himself. The hexagram, with its immediate connection to this mirroring of opposites, was widely used in Alchemy. Today the symbol is often used in connection with the spiritual quest for balance and harmony and is scattered through Freemasonry, Rosicrucianism and the New Age movement, perfectly portraying the oft-quoted axiom, 'as above, so below.'

This association with esoteric or occult thought has run through history as a distinct thread. Dr John Dee, astrologer to Queen Elizabeth I of England, wrote of the hexagram that it is 'the Mystery of Mysteries, a geometrical synthesis of the whole occult doctrine' in his book *Hieroglyphic Monad* in 1564.

The Alchemical symbolism extends even into popular culture, and nowhere more popular than in the brewing of beer. The six-pointed Brewer's Star has been used since mediaeval times to signify purity. Again, we have the 'reconciliation of opposites' used in the brewing process, the fire and water, air and earth. As far back as the 14th Century Europe, the hexagram was used to signify the purity of the beer and the tradition was still extant in 20th Century America.

The hexagram was also the guild mark of the makers of Damascus steel. For centuries swords were marked with the Star of Damascus to show they had been made and 'proved' in that area. Still today the US Navy's swords carry the Star as a symbol of excellence.

The richest vein of history for the hexagram runs through Judaism, however. Perhaps the most emotive usage of the symbol is as the Star of David. Within living memory, Europe has seen Jews branded with the yellow star, incarcerated in the ghettos of the Nazi regime, and slaughtered in their millions in Hitler's concentration camps. The *Magen David* has become synonymous with the horror of the Holocaust. Yet it remains a symbol of faith and unity for the Jewish people.

There are many theories regarding the origin of the Magen David or Shield of David. One theory looks at the physical shield of King David, banded with metal in the shape of a star. Another credible tradition asserts that the shield bore the image of the *Menorah*, the seven-branched candelabra. The design for the original Menorah was said to have been given to Moses by God (Exodus 25: 31-40). It is thought to represent the burning bush where God appeared to Moses on Mount Sinai, and at another level, to symbolise the seven days of Creation. Because of this, the Menorah is believed to signify that God intended a personal relationship with His people.

This bringing together of Man and God, this 'reconciliation of opposites', is equally well reflected in the hexagram with its central point and six rayed star equating to the seven points of the Menorah. That Jews also refer to God Himself in prayers as the Magen David may also provide food for thought.

David, of course, was the father of King Solomon, and the hexagram has become known to many as the Seal of Solomon. While the standard biblical portrayal shows a strong king, legend and ancient folklore and writings associate him with magic and demonology. Many books have been written on the link between Freemasonry and the temple of Solomon, even more have been penned on the magical side.

One thing that is known and documented is that Solomon marries the daughter of an Egyptian Pharaoh. This was highly unusual at the time, as the daughters of the Royal house were not generally given in marriage to rulers of other lands. In Kings 11:4-8 it is told how, as he grew older, Solomon turned from his God at the instigation of his many wives and worshipped Ashtoreth and Moloch amongst others. God became angry and turned away from Solomon, saying "Yea, ye took up the tabernacle of Moloch and the star of your god..." (Acts 7:43). Similarly, Amos 5:26 reads "But you shall carry Sikkut your king, and Kiyyun, your images, the star-symbol of your god which you made for yourself."

Moloch was associated with Fire, and it has been suggested that there is a connection to the Semitic god Ba'al, and the worship of these gods included 'passing children through fire'. This has traditionally been understood to be the sacrifice of children by burning, as in Deuteronomy 12:31 "...for even their sons and their daughters they have burnt in the fire to their gods." However, in Deuteronomy 18:10, we read, "There shall not be found among you anyone that maketh his son or his daughter to pass through the fire, or that useth divination, or an observer of times, or an enchanter, or a witch." This passing through the fire appears rather as a magical act, and there is much debate on the actual meaning of this concept. It may be that children were passed through flame to purify them, and this connects with the myths of Isis and Demeter who held babes in the fire to burn away their mortality and give them eternal life.

Ba'al was a title, equating to 'Lord', rather than the specific name of the God. In Carthage he was worshipped as a ram and called Ba'al Qarnaim (Lord of the Two Horns) at Jebel bu Kornein, the hill of two horns. Ba`alat Gebal, Lady of Byblos, was also associated with Astarte.

The Jewish people already had a history entwined with that of Egypt. Long years the people spent beside the Nile, before Moses, raised as a prince in the court of Pharaoh, led them in search of the Promised Land. It would be unreasonable to suppose that the Hebrew people had not absorbed a knowledge and understanding of the symbols and religion of Egypt. One need only look at the statues of Isis and Horus to be struck by the similarities with depictions of the Virgin and Child. It is perhaps less well known that Ashtoreth, also known as Astarte, is also represented suckling a child as far back at the Eighteenth Dynasty.

If we follow the thread of Solomon's worship back to Ashtoreth, we find that the symbolism associated with the Star takes a curious twist and begins to lead us towards the various manifestations of the Goddess. Remember that in the Mysteries it is said that 'all the gods are One God; all the goddesses are One Goddess.' In other words, there is only the Divine, the Source, the One, by whatever Name we choose to use. The different faces of the gods, their stories, and symbols, are all designed to reflect the Light of a single aspect of a multifaceted jewel.

Ashtoreth was a Canaanite Goddess and seen as the female counterpart of Ba'al. Although biblical references may paint her in a negative light, it must be remembered that the Bible was written from the perspective of one religious' group, and not in a spirit of religious tolerance. Historically, Ashtoreth was seen as a lunar Goddess, and therefore closely associated with the symbolism of Water. Thus, with Ba'al and Ashtoreth, the twin triangles of Fire and Water are apparent.

Ishtar is another name for the Goddess in Babylon, who ruled the morning and evening star. The name derives from the Sumerian meaning 'unique star'.

In Ashkelon, where Herodotus tells of her most ancient temple, she was worshipped as Atar-gatis, a woman with the tail of a fish, thus reinforcing the Water symbolism.

Ashteroth, Astarte, Ishtar, Inanna... all these primary Goddesses can be traced through their associations with the pantheons of later cultures, sharing the same attributes. We can see the origins of Aphrodite and Hera, Juno, and Venus. Love, sex, war, and motherhood.

Ashteroth was also Ishtar, the Babylonian Goddess of the evening star. She was the only Goddess in the pantheon to have equal standing with the Gods and was worshipped under many names and forms. She was seen as Goddess of both love and war and was seen as the creatrix of the universe. The lunar connection gave rise to Ashteroth being symbolised by the horns of a cow. In Genesis 14:5, we are told of a battle, 'And in the fourteenth year came Chedorlaomer and the kings that were with him and smote the Rephaims in Ashteroth Karnaim'. Judas Maccabeus is said to have captured a place in Gilead called Carnaim with a temple of Atar-Gatis. Ashteroth Karnaim means Ashteroth of the Two Horns.

The twin-horned Goddess of Egypt, one of the most beloved of their pantheon and with whom Moses would undoubtedly have been familiar is Hathor. The cow-horned Goddess predates dynastic history, and it is impossible to state how long she has been worshipped. Recent excavations at Nekhen (Heirakonopolis) discovered a trinity interment of bull, cow, and calf, suggesting that even in this earliest Egyptian settlement, the cow-goddess was revered. A stone urn found there depicts a cow with stars on her horns and ears.

Hathor is the Goddess of love, of birth and, as the Mistress of the West, the deity who welcomes the dead. One of the early forms of Hathor was named Mehet-uret, which means the 'great flood', and may refer to her connection with the Milky Way, seen as a waterway of stars in the heavens, and associates her with the waters of birth.

Hathor also appears in Egyptian mythology in a sevenfold aspect. The seven Hathors are depicted as either cows or as seven beautiful young women. The cow form is often depicted as covered with stars and is most associated with Hathor's protection and guiding of the dead, while the female forms were said to attend the birth of children, knowing the length and story of their days. The seven Hathors were worshipped in the Waset (Thebes), Iunu (On, Heliopolis), Aphroditopolis, Sinai, Momemphis, Herakleopolis, and Keset. They may have been linked to the Pleiades, an open cluster of stars in the constellation of Taurus that are often called the Seven Sisters.

The Pleiades cluster features in the mythologies of most cultures worldwide. To the Egyptians they represented Neith, the divine mother and lady of heaven. To the Bronze Age peoples of Europe, their rising on the cross-quarter day between the autumn equinox and the winter solstice which marked the festival of the ancestors, symbolized mourning, and sorrow. In astrology today they are regarded as representing coping with grief. One story tells that Hathor was born in the centre of a lotus from the tears of Ra and the association seems appropriate. In Hindu symbolism, the Pleiades are called the star of fire and the Flames of Agni, the God of Fire.

This once again brings us back to Fire and Water, the two triangles that form the hexagram. Six points and a central seventh. As we journey through this book you will find many correspondences, old and perhaps new, which will give insight into this symbol. Perhaps the most notable glyph you will encounter is the Tree of Life

(Appendix 1), on which the hexagram lights up like a star. However, the Tree is the subject of further exploration and will be covered in a later chapter.

Seven has always been held to be a mystical number. The Bible tells us that God created the world in seven days. There were held to be seven planets, and these are the primary planets used to this day in astrology. There are seven Noble Metals. Seven gateways to the Underworld through which Inanna had to pass. The Alchemists drew the hexagram with a small, seventh point added, to symbolize the presence of God. The list is endless; as is the voyage of discovery this exploration of a single, simple symbol can lead us on.

# The Hexagram and the Elements

The hexagram is merely a symbol. It is a symbol that clearly shows the four Elements of Fire, Water, Air and Earth. It is composed of two interlaced equilateral triangles. One triangle has its single point facing upwards and the other has its single point facing downwards. The first triangle is, of course, a symbol of Fire, and the second triangle is a symbol for Water. The symbols for Air and Earth are also formed by the combination of the Fire and Water triangles in the form of a hexagram (Figure 1). In symbolizing the four Elements, the hexagram is speaking to us of its fundamental hidden message – that of the Totality and the total perfection of the ALL.

*Figure 1: The Hexagram*

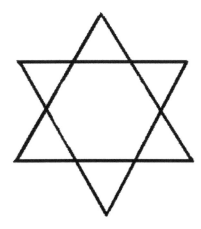

Because of its perfect symmetry, a line drawn horizontally through the center of the hexagram is also a line of reflection. What is above is reflected below (Figure 2) and here the hexagram echoes the great occult maxim – "As above, so below". The symmetry across this axis of reflection shows us that what is above is indeed the mirror image of what is below and *vice versa.* The hexagram is quite often mentioned as a symbol that depicts this 'as above, so below' maxim in occult literature, but that it seems, is where discussion of the hexagram quite often ends.

*Figure 2: Perfect Horizontal Symmetry*

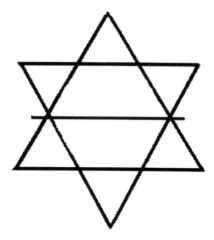

So let us pursue this concept a little further.

The two triangles that make up the hexagram can be also seen as representing God and Man, Fire and Water, Macrocosm and Microcosm, and indeed any number of other reflected pairs or opposites. In the case of God and Man, it is showing that God and Man are reflections of one another. Equally, it shows that the Higher Self and the Lower Self are also reflections of each other. It is here that the hexagram is hinting at its hidden, deeper meanings because, as a symbol of complete balance and harmony, it is suggesting that, in truth, Man and God, Higher self and Lower self should be, were designed to be, reflections of one another. It states quite categorically in our opinion, that Man was indeed created in the image and likeness of God; that the Microcosm reflects the Macrocosm and so on. Indeed, Ye are Gods!

Another line drawn vertically through the hexagram will also form a vertical axis of reflection and so, the hexagram can also be shown to contain the Cross, which once again represents the 4 Elements as the equal armed cross is yet another common symbol for the four Elements (Figure 3). The hexagram also contains two circles, an outer circle drawn completely around its outer points and an inner circle drawn within the center of the Hexagram again hinting at the oneness and totality of the ALL (Figure 4).

*Figure 3: The Equal Armed Cross and the Hexagram*

*Figure 4: The Two Circles*

But let us for a moment again consider the elements Fire and Water. Fire is like spirit, it is like a force or energy, and, in polar terms, it is Active. Consider the Fire triangle with its single point facing upwards and think about that superimposed on a man's body, the two bottom points representing the gonads and the single upright point representing an erect phallus. Note also that physical fire burns upwards almost in the form of a triangle and that heat rises. Fire burns and in doing so it also either transforms or destroys.

Now consider the triangle that represents Water. Water is a reflective liquid that has the power to dissolve. It is a form, and it is Receptive. The water triangle superimposed on a woman's body would have the ovaries as the two upper points and the womb or vagina as the single lower point. Simplistically, when we combine man and woman in sexual union, and we are fortunate, the woman becomes pregnant and will eventually deliver of a child. Symbolically, when the Fire and Water triangles are brought together in a hexagram form, another child is revealed but this child is one that is not ''born of woman.'

On reflection then, the hexagram represents complete polarity. It represents polarity in all its totality and in every direction (horizontal, vertical, and so on). In the center of that totality of all possible polarities, or in the center of the hexagram, is a 'hidden' or perhaps unobvious seventh point that is often overlooked – especially by those who simply tend to regard the hexagram as simply a satanic or evil occult symbol.

Those that see the hexagram as a symbol of evil take their view from the idea that it has six points and hence, they believe that it represents the biblical '666' – the name of the Beast. Funnily enough, there is insight in this too (which we will revisit below) even though they have missed something extremely important in the fact that the hexagram has seven points not six, for in the center of the hexagram, the symbol of utter harmony and balance, is the seventh point. That point is at the very center of its symmetric axes and occupies the point of perfect balance and perfect harmony. It occupies the place of perfection (Figure 5).

*Figure 5: The Seventh Point*

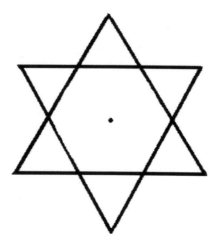

The Pleiades, a group of seven heavenly stars, have also long also been associated with this concept in occult lore. In the book Comte de Gabalis[1], one will find the text of the '*Seven Ancient Prophesies of World Peace*' along with the author's (of the Comte de Gabalis) insightful commentary. We read this prophecy with great interest as we researched the Hexagram and, found the explanation of a reference to the Pleiades extremely relevant. "*The Pleiades were seven in number, six of whom are described a visible and the seventh invisible.*" For the literalist, the hexagram's six points are indeed visible leading them to the mistaken belief that this is a symbol tainted by evil because of its association with '*666*'. But for those who contemplate this symbol in a deeper way and in the context of harmony and balance, the seventh invisible point is suddenly visible, and it is truly remarkable.

One can also equate the six outer points of the hexagram to the six days that God worked on His creation in the book of Genesis. The seventh point in the very center of the hexagram signifies the seventh day, a day of rest. Those who see the hexagram as a satanic or evil symbol only see the six days of toil and not the Sabbath or day of rest represented by that seventh point. They see the six days of action through polarity and not the day of rest in which those polarities are finally reconciled, and the work accomplished.

---

[1] Comte De Gabalis by Abbe N. de Montfaucon de Villars

The hexagram is representative of Man in a state of Godlike perfection because through the six days of toil, through the hard work of reconciling our inner polarities and restoring our inner balance, we arrive finally and only perhaps after many lifetimes, at our true selves. We find our inner spirit, our Holy Guardian Angel. We work the Great Work, and we finally discover that we are eternal beings in a timeless state, and we can truly rest in that eternality.

Now, without appreciation of that hidden seventh point of the hexagram, its real use as an occult (hidden) symbol is lost and then it is indeed perhaps more symbolic of the Fall of Man than of Man's potential for glory as the perfect reflection of God. It becomes a reminder only of what ought to have been, what could have been and therefore, without the central seventh point, it certainly also evokes a comparison with the Devil tarot card. Therefore, we state above that those who see the Hexagram as a symbol of evil have a point, for unless they understand and perceive that the Hexagram truly has seven points and understand the significance of this fact, they see actually just a symbol for imperfection.

The Devil tarot card is representative of the internal nature of Man in disarray. It shows how the conscious and the subconscious aspects of Man, depicted as the Man and Woman on the card, are no longer communicating, no longer connected in a meaningful and proper manner. The Man and the Woman can be seen as two opposites or qualities such as Fire and Water, Sun and Moon, or Spirit and Soul, higher self, and lower self. Connection with the Higher Self has also been lost and, without this element of divine inner guidance, 'Man' appears to be chained to the outer world of 'reality'; chained to that outer world of illusion and the material. We use the word 'appears' because this too is only an illusion aptly demonstrated by the fact the chains of bondage depicted in the tarot card are loose and do not actually bind but simply appear to. The Man, or the conscious self, looks outward into a world of his own illusion, his own creation, but He is not in control of that creation, rather, IT controls him.

Today, I think more than ever, information and misinformation, truth and lies are very difficult to distinguish between. Everyone, it seems, has an agenda. As some might put it, the 'matrix' has become much more complex and entirely more captivating over the last two decades. The truth, as one TV show I used to like would say, is however, out there somewhere…

One of the most difficult aspects of the training of a Magician is the development of the trained mind. Among others I think Dion Fortune was very forthright on this topic and Franz Bardon, was insistent on not just initial training but continual attention to training the mind. In fact, Bardon's initial exercises on this topic are extremely demanding.

The Magician must shut out the 'matrix' or the external world as irrelevant to a large degree. He knows it to be unreliable and almost certainly designed to side track, fool and hold back oneself from the truth. Some occultists use the oft-quoted term of 'sleepers' to describe most people who are totally engaged with this outer so-called reality. I suppose a more modern, internet-related term would be "Sheeple." The Magician knows that the truth can almost certainly only be discovered in the reality of the inside – in those deep moments of mediation and connection with the All or the One. He also learns that often this connection is visual in the form of symbols, which must be unravelled and understood in the same internalized manner.

The importance of the trained mind is to shut out the clutter. To be able to single-mindedly focus on that inner source of wisdom, not only during meditation, but also in our daily life. We learn to listen to our '*intuition*' and we develop confidence in its accuracy or relevance in the process.

The personal struggles with training the mind – with Bardon's exercises – is also reflected in the fact that we often find ourselves worrying deeply and almost unconsciously about all kinds of nonsense – things that we either cannot control or that we imagine might happen. The truth is that even if our mind has received some training it is still unconsciously uncontrolled. We can poorly control our mind when deliberately and consciously trying, but most of the time, we too are sheeple.

And so, Bardon is correct – we must continue to work on training the mind, on concentration, on emptying the mind and keeping it empty until we become adepts at this practice. That, we fear, takes most of us more time than is offered in a single lifetime. But, today, more than ever before in known history, we need to do this – for our own sanity.

In the Tarot, The Devil card is the 15th key and an excellent view of its meaning and symbology may be found in Paul Foster Case's seminal book on the Tarot. 1+5 also equals 6 almost echoing and reinforcing our view that the Hexagram without the seventh inner point both represents disharmony and can be equated with the Devil card.

Meanwhile, the Lovers tarot card shows an entirely different relationship. It shows the conscious self in active communication with the subconscious self and the subconscious self in communication with the higher self. The Angel represents the Holy Guardian Angel or higher self. Notice that the Man looks to the Woman who looks to the Angel. By contrast with the Devil card, this tarot card depicts correct and working balanced inner relationships. The human condition shown by the Lovers tarot card is also the one that the hexagram depicts. The Lovers card is the 6th key, again reinforcing this comparison and analogy.

But back to the four elements for a moment.

The Fire-Water combination is the most obvious one signified by the hexagram and it suggests that Fire and Water are the true Elements reconciled in the Inner Child or central point of harmony and balance – the inner Gold. Fire is the Father and Water is the mother or expressed in another way, '*the Sun is its Father and the Moon its Mother,*' as stated in the Emerald Tablet of Hermes Trismegistus.

According to the somewhat ignored Czech Magician, Franz Bardon, the principle of Fire was the first element to emerge from the Akasha and, as he states[2], "*that is why, at the beginning of any creation, there is Fire and Light. Even the Bible begins with the words: Fiat Lux – Let there be light*". For Bardon, the principle of Water is the opposite of Fire while the element Air he sees as the "*mediator*" between Fire and Water establishing the neutral equilibrium between the two. Earth becomes the last element that emerged from the reciprocal action of the other three. Our hexagram appears to show something like support Bardon's viewpoint in that Fire and Water are the two obvious Elements and it is only when they are placed together in the form of the hexagram that the symbols for Air and Earth become apparent.

During G. Michael Vasey's 5-year studies in the First-Degree course with the SOL, he became acquainted with an inner guide named Asteroth. The full story of his interactions with Asteroth are told in his book *Inner Journeys: Explorations of the Soul* and do not need retelling here except insofar as to credit that contact Asteroth with much of the content of this book. Asteroth, who revealed some of the mysteries of Fire and Water to him, stated quite categorically

---

[2] Initiation Into Hermetics, Franz Bardon

*"Fire is the First Born"*. It is on that very statement that much of the content of this book is based.

In Bardon's book, the elements are opposite to each other, and each element also has its own polarity. While he describes Fire as hot and expansive, he quickly points to the ability of Fire to be constructive, creative, and procreative on the one hand and yet decomposing and destructive on the other. Water he defines by its coldness and contractive capability, which is on one hand constructive, life giving, nourishing, and preserving but on the other decomposing, fermenting, divisive and dispersing. Air, as a product of Fire and Water is both warm and moist but has the positive effect of life giving on one side and being destructive on the other. Finally, Earth represents solidification. Note that in discussing Fire, Water. Air and Earth, both Bardon and we are talking about principles, the 'Elements' and not physical Fire, Water, Air or Earth alone.

For each element triangle in the hexagram, we can immediately see how the two basal points of those triangles represent the polar forces or polar qualities of each element. So, for Fire, the two basal points of the Fire triangle can be 'constructive' and 'destructive' while the third single point on the triangle represents the point of balance or harmony between the two basal points. That third upper single point is the product of the two polar qualities of the lower points and, in the so-called Law of the Triangle; we observe that something new is created at that third upper single point. Just as a triangle can be drawn with Man and Woman as the opposite points and Child as the third singular point of equilibrium or as the product of the two polarities, so too can we see the same in the triangles representing the four Elements.

In fact, implicit in the hexagram are three different directions of polarity,

- The first is the **vertical** polarity represented by the uppermost and lowermost tips of the symbol. This polarity is representative of the Above and the Below, God and Man, Fire and Water, etc. upon which we have already touched.
- The second is **horizontal** polarity represented by the leftmost and rightmost points on the hexagram symbolizing the positive and negative qualities or aspects of the Elements such as constructive and destructive or other opposite qualities such as birth and death, black and white, and so on.
- There is also a third dimensional polarity that we term the 'in-out' or **active** polarity. It is represented only when the hexagram can be seen in 3-D, but it symbolizes action in motion such as push-pull or attract-repel.

The hexagram reflects to us the three dimensions of the actuality in which we live as the opposites and everything in between.

The easiest of these polarities to appreciate is horizontal polarity.

Simply think of opposite qualities such as love and hate, black and white, male, and female, or foolhardiness and cowardice, force, and form, for example. These polar qualities are then reconciled by the Law of the Triangle in the third upper single point. Think of other qualities that are opposites of each other and you have the general idea of horizontal polarity.

Vertical polarity can be considered as reflective. What is above is reflected below but in a less magnificent form! For example, Heaven and Earth, God and Man, Macrocosm and Microcosm and this polarity is alluded to in 'As above, so below'. It can also be thought of as the finer reflected in the more solid or as say Spirit and Material. It gets more complex when one tries to combine the idea of both vertical and horizontal polarity but perhaps, we could use the examples presented to us by the hexagram itself. Let's take the two triangles representing the Elements of Fire and Water and we can take the polar qualities of those as described by Bardon to illustrate the concept.

On the vertical axes of the Fire triangle are the polar qualities of 'constructive, creative and procreative' on one side and 'destructive and decomposing' on the other. These represent the extreme points across the base of the Fire triangle and the upper single third point would reconcile as 'heat and expansion'. Similarly, the polar qualities on the base of our Water triangle are 'life-giving, nourishing and preserving' as one set of qualities and 'decomposing, fermenting, divisive and dispersing' as the other opposite set of qualities. These are reconciled in the lower single third point as 'cold and contracting'.

So far so good? By overlaying our two triangles in the form of the hexagram, we find our vertical polarity automatically as 'heat and expansion' reflected as 'cold and preserving' or put very simply – Fire and Water! Water is the reflection of Fire as Earth is the reflection of Air in vertical polar terms. The triangles' single point resolves into the qualities of Element itself.

Now comes the rather more difficult concept of 'in-out' or active polarity in the third dimension. In a sense, continuing with our example above, it could be termed 'burning-wetting' or 'burning-dissolving'. The polarity is between the action of 'burning' versus the action of 'wetting' or perhaps 'dissolving'. We will revisit the three polarity axes later but for now let's simply agree that all three are alluded to in the hexagram.

As stated above, each set of elemental polarities are balanced in the third singular point and, something is created at that point – a product of the reconciliation of polarities. Asteroth once said to *"Reconcile the Opposites"*. In the hexagram, we have a symbol that denotes the opposites of the four elements and their singular points of equilibrium – their four products. But these are combined in a sort of 'Super Nova' of their vertical, horizontal, and active polarities that are all ultimately reconciled into that single central point on the hexagram. That single inner point (try to view the hexagram in three-dimensions) is the absolute point of harmony, equilibrium, and balance.

To continue with the example based on Bardon's elemental properties, all polarities associated with Fire and Water are ultimately reconciled at that one point and one point alone – that hidden seventh point at the very center of the hexagram. Here we find the total reconciliation of Fire and Water (heat and cold, expansion and contraction), burning and wetting/dissolving and the polar qualities of each element. But what is the product of this reconciliation? In fact, since the two triangles represent the FOUR elements in the hexagram, that inner seventh point represents something that reconciles all four elements – and that can surely only be what is termed the Quintessence or in Bardon's terminology - Akasha.

This point, the hexagram's hidden inner point of total balance and harmony, must also be eternal. It must be a place or rather a state of no motion or action. It must combine all the qualities of the Elements and all the elements, or it combines both the macrocosm and the microcosm. It represents the Great Work of alchemy, the true inner and eternal spark, it is the Sun/Son, and it is the Holy Guardian Angel. It is known as Tiphareth on the Tree of Life, and it is what we truly are in our lower vehicles– eternal reflections of the Creator who is the Sun behind the Sun. The central point of the hexagram is the Child not 'born of Woman' – the Solar Child. It is the eternal reflection of the Creator, the Source, and the Father. It is Tiphareth - the reflection of Kether.

In fact, we can flip this idea somewhat and simply consider a point for a moment. A point is static, and it is therefore timeless and without motion. Eternal. Imagine now an explosion of light (Fire) at that point expanding like a ripple on a pool of water. This ripple has movement, and it requires an additional concept, the concept of time, for the movement to be observed. Both the ripple and the point always exist since time must simply be a creation of the observer that allows for the ripple to have motion. The point is both the origin of the ripple and the sum of the parts of the ripple. The hexagram can be viewed the same way.

The hexagram then might be said to represent the ALL THAT IS and because of its internal symmetry, it represents the ALL THAT IS in perfect harmonious balance – pure perfection. It is a symbol of perfection, but it also suggests that perfection or harmony is something very delicate, immensely fragile, and easily lost. It is something that must be purposely sought for.

The outward idea of six points hiding an internal seventh point in the hexagram also seems to uphold this idea that perfection indeed must be sought out and looked for. As we will show later, the hexagram itself provides all the occult knowledge required to seek out that perfection, to turn the inner relationships depicted in the Devil tarot card into that depicted by the Lovers. In that sense, the act of seeking the seventh hidden point or the invisible star is akin to seeking the even deeper meaning that is implicit in the hexagram itself.

There is much more information in the hexagram regarding the four Elements which we will revisit later. But, to summarize, the hexagram contains the four Elements signified by both the triangle symbols for the Element and as the equal armed cross. It has six obvious 'points' and one hidden 'point' in its heart or center making seven points in total. It represents harmony and perfection, and it reveals the workings of three types of polarity that are ultimately reconciled in its hidden seventh point.

# The Hexagram and the Tree of Life

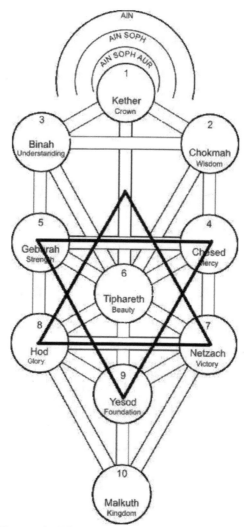

*Figure 6: The Hexagram on the Tree of Life*

The next step in our analysis of the hexagram is to overlay it quite simply onto the Tree of Life (Figure 6). The Tree of Life is a glyph or diagram that shows the arrangement of ten interconnected spheres (called sephirah or sephiroth (plural)) representing the organizational system of the Jewish Kabbalistic tradition. The Tree of Life is variously thought of as a map of the universe and of the psyche, a depiction of the order of the creation of the cosmos, and a path to spiritual illumination. The ten spheres are connected by paths, which are assigned to the twenty-two letter-numbers of the Hebrew alphabet. It is a mystical map of how the world works, how the person works and how life works. Each of the ten spheres has a name that directly identifies the sephirah and the ideas that each sephirah represents. The various names of the sephiroth are derived from Scripture.

The Tree of Life depicts the ten emanations of God moving progressively down the Tree in the path of creation from the most esoteric point of manifestation to the emanation of God in physical reality. Each sephirah is considered as holy as all the others irrespective of its position since the whole tree represents God and his creation. As a result, our physically manifest life is just as holy and as worthwhile as our spiritual life.

The Tree of Life can also be used as a reference guide to creation since each sephirah and each path on the Tree may be associated to some set of correspondences such as Tarot cards, the planets or virtually any other system. It can be used as a vast filing cabinet of exoteric and esoteric information providing a way for the student to access that information.

When the Hexagram is placed on the Tree of Life one will immediately observe that it fits very neatly into place with the upper point of the Fire triangle equating to Daath, the invisible sephirah, the lower point of the Water triangle equating to Yesod, the two left hand points of the Fire and Water triangles equating to Geburah and Hod and, the two right hand points of the Fire and Water triangles equating to Chesed and Netzach. The central seventh point now sits, rather aptly, over Tiphareth. Placed in this manner on the Tree, the hexagram proves to be a key that unlocks a great deal of additional information that helps us to understand relationships within the Tree.

Interestingly, in gematria the value of Daath is 474, which adds up to 6 (4+7+4=15, 1+5=6). Daath is the highest point of awareness of a human soul. There are 6 sephiroth in the world of formation and in numerology, 6 is taken as the number of perfect union. It is representative of unfoldment, growth, and nurturing. The number 7 is taken as the number of perfection, mysticism, and understanding.

The first thing to note is that the base of the Fire triangle joins the sephiroth Hod and Netzach to reconcile at Daath while the Water triangle joins the sephiroth Geburah and Chesed to reconcile at Yesod. Tiphareth is the seventh point inside the center of the hexagram. Now the first issue to address is likely to be the status of Daath. Sometimes called the eleventh sephirah, it really isn't a sephirah at all, but we like to think of it as the effect of Kether, Chokmah and most importantly, Binah, combined for the purposes of examining the hexagram. For now, let's just accept that and move on since we will revisit this later in more detail.

What is fascinating when overlaying the hexagram on the Tree is to study some of the other details that readily emerge. For example, the common attribution of the elements with the Sephiroth is as follows,

Netzach – Fire

Hod – Water

Chesed – Water

Geburah – Fire

Notice then that the basal two points on the Fire triangle are attributed to Water (Hod) and Fire (Netzach) again recalling the polarity of the element Fire discussed in the previous chapter. Likewise, the upper two points of the Water triangle are also attributed to Water (Chesed) and Fire (Geburah). Furthermore, when the horizontal plane of symmetry is added, we observe that the symmetry is also maintained in the elemental attributions of the Sephiroth.

Interestingly, the base of the Fire triangle also equates to the 27<sup>th</sup> path (Peh, Mouth) on the Tree, which once again is usually also attributed to the element of Fire. Just to pile on for the moment, if the two outer points on either side of the hexagram are joined by the Paths on the tree we again find that on the left hand side that Path is the 23<sup>rd</sup> Path (Mem, Water) attributed to Water and on the right hand side is Path 21 (Kaph, Grasping Hand) attributed to Fire; showing that the symmetry of the hexagram in the vertical plane holds in a certain fashion. But if we also examine the line of vertical symmetry, we find that the Path from Yesod to Tiphareth, the 25<sup>th</sup> Path (Samekh, Prop), is attributed to Fire and the Path from Tiphareth through Daath, the 13<sup>th</sup> Path (Gimel, Camel) is attributed to Water.

The hexagram placed this way on the Tree of Life seems indeed to be a perfect fit.

## *Polarity on the Tree*

Implicit in the Tree of Life, as in the hexagram, is polarity. It seems to us that polarity is often thought of as force and form, male and female, black and white, life and death and so on, but this is only *one* aspect of polarity, and it is that aspect that is represented from left to right on the Tree of Life – what we have termed horizontal polarity. The second form of polarity, represented from top to bottom of the Tree, is from spiritual to material, from eternal light to the temporary darkness of night and from the eternal to the temporally constrained – is what we call vertical polarity.

Let's consider that last idea in a bit more detail. Firstly, let's assume that Kether already exists – and let's discuss the Tree of Life in terms of developing an idea or a concept and turning it into reality. Kether is the source but as the Tree unfolds down into Malkuth, things become more set in stone, more constrained by the rules we created along the way. Yes- the Tree contains an unknowable number of possibilities but how does it work?

If one has an idea and sets out to turn that idea into reality, we go through several steps. First, we have the Idea itself – the Eureka moment. But to have an idea, we must have some form of drive to think and ponder, and we must have some concept of turning an idea into more than an idea. So, we are already through Chokmah and Binah by the time we have the idea; we must be since Chokmah provides the desire to create and Binah provides us with the concept of forms. Without these, we can't possibly have an idea since I simply AM – Kether.

Let's imagine our idea is to design and build a house. We must first have the idea of a form of shelter that we will call a house – this is my Eureka moment, and it must take place in Chesed. As my idea gets further refined in all its details, each is tested, thought through and considered and it is either accepted or discarded (Geburah) and then as we go down the remainder of the tree we are polishing, adding further details and solving problems as they arise. Finally, we have our blueprint for the house (Yesod) and must now take that blueprint and turn it into reality via a construction project (Malkuth).

None of this is truly a mystery but the further into the process we go, the more constrained our reality is becoming. When we started with the original idea, our house could have been anything, made of anything, look like anything and so on, but by the time we are complete, we have something and that something was constrained utterly by the decisions we made and the laws we formulated to calculate issues like load factors, number of rooms, location of the boiler and so forth.

So, our living reality is also constrained by 'laws'. The Creator of that reality created those laws and reality is constrained to what it is. Free will was a part of the process of moving down the Tree but, in the end, the step between Yesod and Malkuth doesn't really include much free will anymore because we have so bound ourselves within our own constraints. As Asteroth said, *"There is consequence in Action"*. That consequence is that as we create, we both constrain and limit our creation. We create rules, laws, and formulations to construct something real and tangible on the material level.

Which brings us back to the concept of time.

In Kether, a point of being, there is no time – it is timeless and eternal – it simply IS. It is simply I AM. But as soon as we start to move down the Tree, as soon as we create the idea of dimensions, our single point becomes a line between two points. One point becomes an unlimited number of points along a vector or direction. In other words, our being now has movement and in having movement we must have a concept in which we can observe such movement – TIME. Time is therefore a construct. It is a constraint on which our reality is based. Time does not exist because I simply AM. I simply EXIST. But to start the process of creation, we need a rule, a marker, an angle with which to experience and that is time. Time is a thus a basic constraint on our reality (as is space).

The idea of creating something and needing to become more constrained to do so is perhaps nothing new, but it is a form of polarity represented on the Tree of Life. We call it vertical polarity by contrast with the other types of polarity (horizontal polarity such as black and white, male, and female etc. and active polarity) that we usually think about as polarity. So, going back to the hexagram, we have already observed there is both horizontal polarity and vertical polarity and, of course, that these axes of polarity neatly correspond to the lines of reflection in the Hexagram that we discussed in the last chapter where we discussed our concept of active polarity.

On the Tree of Life, horizontal polarity is somewhat obvious, and we refer to the three 'pillars' as the extremes of polarity (the pillar of Severity and the pillar of Mercy) and the balance in between (the Middle pillar or pillar of balance). In a sense, vertical polarity is also referred to via the concept of the four worlds (Atziluth, Briah, Yetzirah and Assiah) which infer a process from eternal spark through to creation in a constrained physical creation as discussed above.

Vertical polarity is from spiritual to physical. There is also a vague concept perhaps of active polarity because the Tree of Life is really a three-dimensional structure and not a two-dimensional diagram but, because it is naturally presented as a two-dimensional diagram, that active polarity is often lost to us. Visualizing the hexagram as two interlocked pyramids, like the merkabah figure, helps us to conceptualize the three polarities as horizontal and vertical plus depth. In a two-dimensional representation we observe on horizontal and vertical polarities, and we do not see the polarity offered by depth.

When we place the hexagram upon the Tree of Life, these polar relationships come back strongly into focus. Horizontal polarity can be observed via the Law of the Triangle in our elemental triangles while vertical polarity is observed via the As Above – So Below relationship and that active or in/out polarity, while still not as obvious, becomes clearer too – it is action/inaction.

## The Three Cycles

Placing the Hexagram on the Tree of Life also suggests some other relationships that are combinations of the polarities discussed above which we will refer to as 'cycles.'

### The Cycle of Potential

Let us start with the relationship between Hod and Chesed where a line can be drawn from one Sephirah to the other passing through Tiphareth. We will call this the "Cycle of Potential" as Chesed provides both order and a framework for formulation and discrimination. It helps set constraints on our personal realities whereas Hod provides fluidity, and is related to our habits as well as learning, communication, and trade. Path 20 and Path 26 through the Hexagram join the two. Path 20 is essentially about the structure of all that is formed, and Path 26 relates to how new forms are created. So here we have a relationship that incorporates all three aspects of polarity and presents us with a view on our potential to create. The seed of our creative instincts reside in Chesed, but they are influenced heavily by our habits and current perceptions at Hod. This truly is the basis of our potential as humans and our ability to create. It is also intriguing to note that both Hod and Chesed, despite being on opposite pillars on the Tree, are both attributed to Water.

### *The Cycle of Action*

The second cycle is the "Cycle of Action" which is observed in the line drawn through the Hexagram from Geburah to Netzach. In Geburah, we find the principle of active change. It is truly the engine room of creation in that it is the great purifier breaking down anything that cannot truly be sustained. In Netzach we find our motivation and drive, our creative urge. Paths 22, which helps increase spiritual powers, and Path 24 link the two, which help provide an appreciation for creation. This cycle then, is about the cycle of creation and destruction, and its reflection in our own psyche. Again, both Geburah and Netzach, despite being on opposite pillars on the Tree, are attributed to Fire.

## The Cycle of Creation

Finally, the last line drawn through the Hexagram speaks to the "Cycle of Creation" and incorporates only vertical polarity as it is drawn from Daath to Yesod and incorporates Path 13 and Path 25. Daath is the gateway from one level of reality to another whereas Yesod is represents the framework on which our reality is built. In that way they are the extreme edges of that level of consciousness in which we can create our reality. Interestingly, this suggests that we do not create our reality *in* Malkuth where it manifests. This is the way of creation.

## The Fire Triangle on the Tree

The Fire triangle unites Hod and Netzach but what does that really tell us? Netzach is attributed to Fire and is a 'force' sephiroth while Hod is attributed to Water and is a 'form' sephiroth. An appraisal of what has been written about these two sephiroth by occultists such as Gareth Knight, Dion Fortune and others is helpful here. They both represent the first 'multitude' and of course are best understood in studying their relationship with one another as a pair. Meditation on these sephirah in the context of the hexagram seems to bring out a somewhat different or rather additional perspective however described below.

Netzach is about emotions and feelings. It is about desire, drive, and instinct. The attribution of Venus reinforces this concept, and it can be said that desire is like *"the fire that burns within us"*. Emotions and feelings are the watery aspect of Netzach, which of course contains its own polarity, but desire... desire is like fire. As Asteroth said, *"Emotion burns like Fire."* It is the alchemical Fire, the hidden secret, and an aspect of the primordial Fire. It is the creative urge. Drive and motivation are based upon desire and desire can be hot and as we all know; it can also burn out of control. Control of the emotions, the drives and urges inside of us ensures that we utilize the energies of Netzach appropriately, but too much or too little emotional drive can result in someone who is either hot-headed or a cold fish! Netzach is often also attributed to the alchemical phase of Fermentation. Fermentation is a process that generates heat and transforms the fermenting mixture into something useful, something better. Netzach represents that multitude of, often conflicting, inner forces that drive our personality to action – for better or for worse.

On the other hand, Hod can be taken to reflect habits, traits, learning and trade. These have a fluid nature but again, the polarity of these characteristics can result in a person who is a slave to habits on one hand or who has no structure to their lives at all on the other. Hod is the myriad of forms and can represent self-awareness and freedom of choice. But, as Asteroth related, it can become the hardening of the life force through loss of innocence. *"The horny material that represents the hardened matter of one's personal life."* From an alchemical point of view, it is often attributed to the distillation phase in which one dissolves something in water to further purify and improve it. Hod represents that multitude of forms of activity that are in essence the outcome of the myriad of personal drivers originating in Netzach. These are often automatic, repetitious, and impulse led, but they ought to be driven by the Higher self and the alignment of our Will with that of the eternal spark, the primordial Fire.

In the context of the Fire triangle, Hod and Netzach can be seen also to represent our experiences. The who we are that is based on our fiery desires and other watery habits as well as the hardened horn of our life experience and hopefully, the motivation to be something, someone better. For us, their location on the Fire triangle suggests the idea of burning up who we are. In essence burning off our life experiences, our over or underdeveloped desire and motivations, and our slavery to habit and automatic responses. We replace this self with one that has a sense of motivated purpose that can utilize our experiences positively and develop freedom from ingrained habits and responses. It suggests that we literally throw ourselves on the fire to purify, and transform whom we are into something more refined, more spiritual, more attuned with the Higher self. For these aspects of ourselves we reconcile the opposites with Fire. We transform through Fire.

Daath is at the upper tip of the Fire triangle. It is of course not a true sephirah at all, being a position on the middle pillar placed on the Abyss. Its virtue is the perfection of justice and the application of virtues untainted by personality or ego and its spiritual experience is the Vision across the Abyss. What a perfect description of the process of burning away the experiences of life, the habits of the ego and ego-driven desires.

The base of the Fire triangle is the 27th Path on the Tree of Life. It, too, is attributed to Fire and most usually to the Tower tarot card and the Hebrew word PEH or mouth. Imagine if you were truly able to transform yourself via Fire in this way, the Tower of your ego would erode, and collapse and it might feel truly catastrophic from the point of view of the ego. The Mouth is the organ of speech and as such it often speaks egotistically or selfishly, and its words are those of our desires, self-motivations, self-deceptions, and experiences of life.

The Fire triangle as a part of the hexagram placed on the Tree of Life echoes the idea of the comparison between what we ought to be, or have the potential to be, and what we are. But and perhaps more importantly, it again seems to point and guide, providing instruction on what is required to enable such a personal transformation. It suggests a process by which we can achieve personal transformation.

## The Water triangle on the Tree

Considering the sephiroth and paths linked by the Water triangle on the Tree also provides much for meditation and thought. The Water triangle combines Chesed, Geburah and Yesod and the base of the inverted triangle is Path 19 attributed to Air. Chesed is on the pillar of force and Geburah on the pillar of form, Chesed attributed to Water and Geburah to Fire. Chesed and Geburah are like the engine room of creation with Chesed spinning out concepts, which are tested, refined, or rejected in Geburah.

Chesed, or Mercy, is associated with the virtue of obedience, but the vices of gluttony, hypocrisy and bigotry, and its' spiritual experience is the vision of love. It is also the first sephirah of action and is the initiator of action – the spark behind action - and where the first concept of forms is produced. It is the creative urge or instinct. It is the seed of an idea that may or not become something. It is the first sephirah below the abyss and the first manifestation of the human consciousness as it corresponds to the intellectual mind. It provides the archetypal ideas and concepts that may form the basis of reality – your reality. It is also the sephirah of governance and the rule of law providing a framework for formulation – the law as a reflection of the constraints of creation – your creation.

Geburah is often thought of as the destroyer but, it is a tester of ideas and proto forms, and while those found wanting are destroyed while those found worthy continue their journey into reality - into actuality. It is also about resolve and energy – the energy to protect and defend what is right, but the ability to be ruthless about what is not. It is the energy behind change and the breaks down old systems of behavior. It is about will and the alignment of will and, according to Asteroth, it is the *"purifying fire"*.

Yesod is the framework of reality. A subtle dimension moulded through thought and imagination that can ultimately be replicated in some fashion in the physical world. It has a fluid-like quality and one can imagine the Sun of Tiphareth reflected in the pool of Yesod as the Moon.

The Water triangle therefore is suggestive of permeating concepts, ideas, and beliefs that are tested and refined, rather like the Blacksmith beats the metals he works with until they take on the form and properties he desires. These refined concepts and ideas find fluid substance in the imagination of Yesod – in the waters of the subconscious where they can finally take root in your reality. The Water triangle then represents our creative processes, and it is perhaps no coincidence that the base of the water triangle is also the Path to which the tarot card Strength is often assigned. It too suggests a process. One of quenching and washing. The blacksmith constantly works his metal in heat and then uses water to quench it, while the idea of washing is expressed well in baptism and the washing away of sin.

## Summary

The Hexagram, when placed on the Tree presents another way to examine multiple relationships and polarities and it is a key of sorts to unlocking much from the Tree about polarity and about our own inner make up and creative process – about our personality, both as it is and as it should be. It suggests practical approaches to refine and purify, to wash and clean ourselves. While this chapter has covered some of these relationships and potential meanings the reader may well benefit from their own contemplation on these relationships.

# The Hexagram and Other Attributions

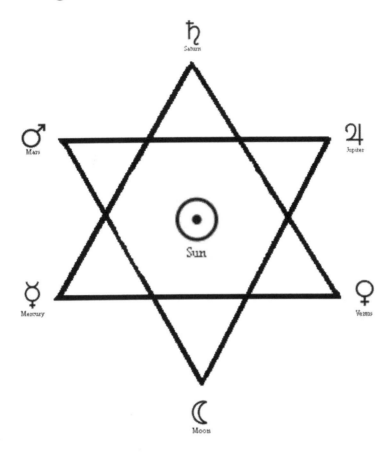

The seven planets and metals, of course, can also be related to the hexagram (Figure 7). The addition of the Metals and Planets to the points of the Hexagram really adds more contexts and more color to what we have already discussed. The Metal/Planet pairings are generally accepted as follows:

- Saturn/Lead
- Jupiter/Tin
- Venus/Copper
- Moon/Silver
- Mercury/Mercury
- Mars/Iron
- Sun/Gold

We can take the diagram of the hexagram on the Tree of Life and add in the Planet/Metal combinations, as shown in Figure 7, as follows,

- Saturn/Lead - Daath
- Jupiter/Tin - Yesod
- Venus/Copper - Chesed
- Moon/Silver - Netzach
- Mercury/Mercury - Hod
- Mars/Iron - Geburah
- Sun/Gold – Tiphareth

By adding in the metals and planet attributions, even greater clarity is offered which we will discuss later. Before doing so however, let's revisit the idea of a point exploding outwards as a concentric circle of light or energy that moves away from that point through time. Draw this and note that you have drawn the symbol for Gold or the Sun – a dot within a circle. Imagine that as the concentric circle moves outwards, six points form on that concentric circle that will form the points of the Hexagram and imagine that each of these points is a planet/metal combination. In essence, have we not just reversed the alchemical process for making Gold? We have taken the central 'gold' and split it into the six other metals. We have taken the Sun and decomposed it into the six other planets. Additionally, those six points that form the Hexagram remain points on a circle – the outer circle of the symbol for Gold or the Sun inferring that it is still involved. We can accept therefore, that all the metals are involved in Gold, and that all the planets are involved in the Sun, as if they were not, we could not decompose them so.

We can also reverse this process and imagine the six planets and metals returning to the center to once again be transmuted into the Sun or Gold. In visualizing this process, we are visualizing part of the process of creation as described both by physics and by the Tree of Life. We are also visualizing a view of the Great Work thus once again – as above, so below. We are visualizing here the hexagram within a circle (Figure 4 above).

## The Planets and Metals

The planets and the metals can be looked at in terms of their traditional attributes and attributions, as well as in terms of their actual physical properties. These attributes and occult properties can be found in the literature and there is no need to dwell on them here except to provide a sufficient summary to make our point. Below are some common attributions:

## *Saturn/Lead*

The planet Saturn is the slowest planet in the solar system, and it usually symbolizes inertia, weight, and stubbornness. It is both materialistic and melancholic. Old man time with his scythe and crutch is often used as an image of Saturn. Saturnalia was the feast that commemorated the dedication of the temple to the god Saturn and involved turning social status upside down for a period whereby slaves became masters and vice versa. The Romans identified Kronos (Father Time) with Saturn, and He taught humans the arts of agriculture. His was the golden age of humanity during which peace and happiness endured until Jupiter overthrew him. Saturn the planet and Saturn the God are both usually associated with Binah.

The metal Lead is the heaviest of the seven metals. It is highly durable and resistant to change; it does not corrode nor rust. It is very soft but brittle and dull. It is impermeable to light and to x-rays and inert with a low melting point. Lead has a sealing off, protective function and brings action to a standstill such as in the printing process or in painting with lead-based paint.

## Jupiter/Tin

Jupiter is associated with beneficial energies and things like luck, idealism, and success. It is believed to influence the mind or higher spirituality. It is also associated with expansion, joviality, and fluency.

Tin is often associated with being practical and unemotional or superficial. It is preserving and is used as a food preservative and in tin cans and in the form of tin foil, gives contour to existing form and adds form staying capabilities in bronze. Surprisingly enough if tin is heated it becomes harder and more brittle, unlike other metals.

## Moon/Silver

The Moon is associated with our emotional functions and the forces that build up the character traits. It is thought of as the seat of the personality and physical expressions and has dominion over form and the night.

Silver is also reflective like the Moon. It captures images as photographs or reflections as in a mirror and in doing so it requires light. In a mirror, the silver is invisible, and you see only the reflection of yourself and your surroundings.

## Mercury/Mercury

The planet Mercury represents the androgynous link between the Sun and the Moon and is also linked with communication and freedom of choice.

The metal is a heavy metal, being both a solid and a liquid that does not wet its surroundings. It is a strange metal but is often also associated with the mind and intelligence, hence the expression 'quicksilver'. The androgynous aspect of the metal is that most other metals may be dissolved in it, and it is therefore amalgamating.

## Mars/Iron

Mars is the planet of desire and war. It is a red planet often associated with male deities and it is active. Iron is the metal often used for the weapons used in war and it is also found in the blood spilled in war. Iron is a common metal that can often be seen in reddish soil or rocks that have a high iron content. Iron also burns and is used in sparklers and so on to provide visual effects. Males have higher concentrations of iron in their blood. Iron is also a key part of the process of oxygenating the body.

## Venus/Copper

Venus is the planet of love and beauty, and it is often associated with a pantheon of Goddesses and is thought of as passive. Interestingly, Copper is also found in the blood but there is 20% more of it in female blood and the Copper level in blood varies with the menstrual cycle.

It is a soft and appealing metal visually both as the metal and as an ore which is often blue or green in color. It is used for jewelry and for parts of buildings where it can be visually appealing such as copper roofs and so on. It is a superb conductor of electricity and used extensively for this purpose.

## Sun/Gold

The Sun is the radiance in our solar system that provides the heat and energy we need to survive. Gold is traditionally the noblest of metals, pure, incorruptible, and malleable, prized as the basis for currency and wealth, and its beauty. It is the color of the Sun.

Let us now revisit the three cycles discussed above in the light of the planets and metals.

In the "Cycle of Potential" we have a relationship that is about our potential to create. Chesed is equated with Jupiter and with Tin as expansion, growth, success, and prosperity, amongst others. It is about increased expansion, extension and, preservation as well as being practical and unemotional. Hod, as Mercury the planet and Mercury the metal, is about the concrete mind, our various faculties and communication. It is about communicating, engaging, and associating. Our potential to create therefore, is based on our ability to grow and 'expand' our reality with our concrete mind, our ability to communicate, and our level of self-awareness. Again, this truly is the basis of our potential as humans and our ability to create our own reality.

In the "Cycle of Action" from Geburah to Netzach, we can add Mars and Iron at Geburah, and Venus and Copper at Netzach. We have the principle of force, will and desire or action and mobilization then at Geburah, and our personal ideals, goals, and values at Netzach. Venus represents our capacity to appreciate, interpret, and give meaning to our life experiences. Iron at Geburah reminds one of an iron fist used to destroy unwanted ideas, constraints, and concepts. Mars reinforces this idea as warlike and spilling the blood of false concepts. Iron and Copper also express the concept of male and female polarity. Again, this cycle is about the cycle of creation and destruction, and its reflection in our psyche.

Saturn and Lead at Daath, and Moon and Silver at Yesod, can represent the "Cycle of Creation" from Daath to Yesod. We have the principle of limitation and definition or form and structure then at Daath and our imaginative faculties, mood, and passivity at Yesod. We imagine our reality as a framework that is constrained by the rules that we have created for it. We can also think of Lead atop the Fire triangle being melted by its heat and the silver at the base of the Water triangle as reflective as Water. Again, this is the way of creation. It suggests that creation is about constantly reflecting on and refining who we are.

However, we must also consider that the seven planets are essentially our inner stars of power. The six outer planets and single inner planet (Sun) represent our make-up, our psyche, in the same way that that portion of the Tree of Life conjoined by the hexagram does.

In fact, if the Hexagram represents the Totality of the All, then so must these seven metals or planets be another view of the human psyche in its totality. We can consider that ideally the six planets all emanated from the one and can be transmuted through work back into that one. Or at least we must seek to understand and control their influences over us.

This latter point takes us back to Bardon. Bardon's initial exercises include what he calls work on two soul mirrors. He asks the student to consider and document all the negative aspects of themselves and then all the positive aspects. He then has the student attempt to group these by their attribution to one of the four elements and by importance. In fact, the Bardon exercise is not a one-off activity but should be continually revisited and reappraised.

What Bardon is doing through this exercise is related to the discussion of the Hexagram in that he is making the student first become aware of his or her own characteristics – negative and positive – through expression of how the four elements manifest themselves in the student's nature. The student is then set to a lifetime task of controlling and reconciling the elements within himself. This is the Great Work and it also another aspect of a trained mind.

The hexagram signifies the Great Work of Alchemy. It signifies the emanated and the source. It is the ALL and its creation or reality. As the symbol of the Sun, it emphasizes this idea that all originated from the Sun or central point, and all will eventually come back to the central Sun. The Hexagram represents the opposites that we must reconcile back to the single point.

It is the six days of work using polarity and the seventh day of rest in which those polarities are reconciled.

## The Three Cycles Revisited

If we look at all of this in a certain way (Figure 8), we immediately observe further associations that we might make. The Cycle of Creation can be seen as the equivalent of alchemical Salt being about the form aspect, the body, and creation. The Cycle of Potential can also be associated with the alchemical principal of Mercury, being about the soul, the passive aspect, the water of life, and the potential to create. Finally, the Cycle of Action can be associated with the alchemical principal of Sulphur, the active fire, the spirit, the cycle of creation, and destruction.

The three cycles, in fact, echo Bardon's training methods in which he states that "*it is impossible to acquire and maintain the magical equilibrium if the body, soul and spirit are not trained simultaneously*". It tells us then that our Great Work must incorporate all three aspects of ourselves.

In fact, in examining the Hexagram, one could probably go much further and include the Chakras and other systems. We will not do so here simply because we do not feel qualified to do so, and we do not wish to mislead the reader through our errors. What can be said is that the Hexagram as a symbol seems to offer a framework in which to compare different systems and strands of occult thought and correlate them all, including alchemy, into a unified system of self-initiation.

## *Summary*

The hexagram as a glyph seems to unify many occult systems in that it brings to the surface several similar messages or meanings across all the systems considered. It appears to point the way and to suggest an approach to the Great Work. It is also a symbol that implies something about the nature of reality and how that can be created by each one of us. Perhaps, properly, these two things are one and the same for in working the Great Work our ability to create reality properly is enhanced. One becomes the great magician; one becomes a god- that is what we were created to be.

### Figure 8: The Three Cycles

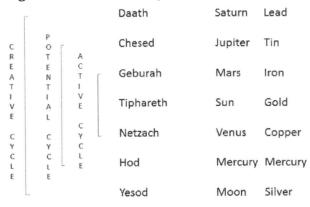

|  |  |  | Daath | Saturn | Lead |
|---|---|---|---|---|---|
| C R E A T I V E | P O T E N T I A L | A C T I V E | Chesed | Jupiter | Tin |
|  |  |  | Geburah | Mars | Iron |
|  |  |  | Tiphareth | Sun | Gold |
| C Y C L E | C Y C L E | C Y C L E | Netzach | Venus | Copper |
|  |  |  | Hod | Mercury | Mercury |
|  |  |  | Yesod | Moon | Silver |

# Using the Hexagram

The Hexagram can be used to reconcile many occult systems and in doing so, it is a key to showing that each system is designed consistently and with a similar purpose. They each show us how to achieve the Great Work of alchemy. The Hexagram shows in multiple different ways that we were created to create. It also shows us that in our current state we are unable to create perfection as we should, because we are unbalanced and out of harmony.

The Hexagram also reveals the importance of polarity. It suggests that there are at least three forms of polarity as discussed previously and in some tenuous way these may be linked with the three alchemical principals. We must always reconcile the opposites. To truly create in a perfect manner, we must reconcile our own internal opposites. We must clean and purify ourselves, set aside the ego, and act in compliance with the will of the All. In that regard, the hexagram also suggests an approach to doing exactly that.

Let us think more about the nature of reality and how it might be that we can make magic. Let us briefly examine the context for all of this by asking the question: What is reality?

Rosicrucian's talk of both 'reality' and 'actuality'. They define reality as essentially what you can perceive about the actuality.

Actuality most likely cannot ever be known. You can only determine your personal reality of actuality, but this reality is actually an illusion. A self-made illusion. For example, time is both a reality and an illusion. It is simply a construct of the mind that is required by the Law of the Universal Mind, to allow for movement and experience. Reality – your reality – is created via the imagination and your belief system. Your culture, upbringing, beliefs and yes- the rules you live life by – all go into creating your reality. But that reality is an illusion – a wakeful dream. It is not *actuality*. All of us fall into the trap of believing in this reality and we all work magic, as the basis of magic is the creation of reality via our belief and imagination. Belief is faith and it really does move mountains because it helps us to create reality.

We know that everything we experience is experienced in our brain. Everything that we see, feel, or hear is experienced via our brain's ability to interpret our environment. This is science. So, what we believe to be on the outside is in fact, inside of us. The real part of me is simply consciousness and what that is from a scientific point of view, is still something of a mystery. Not being quantum physicists, we don't wish to go too far with an analysis of what actuality might be, but there does seem to be a school of thought that says that everything is energy and that it takes the observation of a conscious being to collapse that waveform into particles and matter. In plain English, we create reality through the act of observation.

If everything really is inside of us or, our experience of our environment is inside of us, then logic suggests that we must create this reality as an interpreted image of actuality – whatever that may be. Herein lies the basis of magic. If, we can consciously influence our reality using natural laws, then we can make magic. Both mystical magic in that we can change ourselves via the will, and physical magic in that we can cause an effect in our environment beyond ourselves.

Of course, there are all kinds of implications to these simplest of statements. However, if we wish to be able to perform this magic then we must first and foremost know ourselves. If we observe our reality, then do we not create it? <u>Want to change your reality? Change yourself.</u> Change the way you see things, think about things. Change your internals. Because the act of observing doesn't take place 'out there' but inside of you.

We all probably spend a lot of time trying to figure out the 'truth'. The problem is that for every 'truth' there appears to be several alternatives. 'Truth', it seems, is difficult if not impossible to pin down. Even if one consults the Bible there are any number of alternate interpretations and contradictions. Many occult texts are deliberately obtuse and opaque. So, how are we ever supposed to gain insight into 'truth' whatever that may prove to be? We think there is only one way, and it is that to know the truth in the outside world one must first know the truth in your inner world. If you can come to know yourself – the truth of whom you truly are - then the outer truth is evident. The difficulty is in "*knowing oneself*".

As an example, when we interact with someone and dislike them, it's really because in that person we see the reflection of something we dislike or fear about ourselves. We constantly measure others by projecting ourselves onto them. Our ego doesn't allow us to see this for what it really is. Our views, our beliefs, and our conditioning are used to synthesise and process our view of the other person and find them wanting in some way. Indeed, we may violently disagree with them and see them as our 'enemy'. However, if we truly know ourselves, understand ourselves, and see ourselves for what we really are, then it surely becomes clear to us that we are a child of light, imperfect but evolving with life's lessons to a higher place in that eternal process of evolution.

If I know myself then I recognize my ego for what it truly is and I place it to one side and tell it that I, the real me, I am in charge here! If I can learn to accept myself through self-knowing and coming to terms with who, and what I really am then I learn to love myself. In learning to love myself I can love others through acceptance of what they are and where they are at in their own journey. Acceptance is a process of letting go and as we let go, we no longer feel the need to struggle. We forgive ourselves and we forgive others, and we learn how to truly love. It is only when we truly know and love ourselves that we really gain the right and ability to guide others knowing how to help and correct without damaging that person's self-worth and progress. Otherwise, any act may be based on something less than love; it may be based on our distorted perspective of ourselves.

The Hexagram provides us the tools and insights that we need to begin the work. It provides both reassurance that we can become who were meant to be and a mechanism for getting there. The message is clear. We must start by reconciling the opposites, knowing ourselves and acting in coordination with Universal Law. We must both seek the inner gold that is already there as well as transmute the other metals within us to gold. In doing so, we create a reality that is based not on our egotistical view or inherited cultural view of reality but on the actuality of reality. And once we can do that, once we have understood the Laws and Forces of that reality – we can change that reality at will if we desire. We are the Creator, and we were created in our Creators' image.

# Further Thoughts

It is our belief that the hexagram can be used to reconcile many occult systems. We have examined the elements, the tree of life, the planets, and the metals in some detail in earlier chapters. Though we don't necessarily know as much about astrology, the idea of The Great Year does seem to resonate within the hexagram as well.

The hexagram has six points, of course, but it also has six spaces in between those six points. The sum of the six points and six spaces between the points is twelve. Since the hexagram is the symbol of the Sun, one would imagine that the twelve astrological Sun signs could be arranged around the hexagram in those twelve locations. When we do this, Aquarius is placed at the top of the Fire triangle and Leo at the tip of the downward facing water triangle, and every other sign can then be arranged between them. Now, let us examine the common attributions of the planets to the astrological Sun signs and for the 6 points there is perfect compliance such as Saturn/Aquarius, Aries/Mars, Gemini/Mercury etc., but only to the six signs allocated to the points. Next, take the progression of the Great Year over 26,500 odd years and understand that the circumference of the hexagram represents that Great Year and that each point/space is a Great Month. Again, as the symbol of the Sun, the hexagram is also representative of the Great Year.

Not really being up to speed with astrology, it does seem to us from this rudimentary analysis that the hexagram once again reconciles astrology with other systems and, by using the hexagram as a key, much could be gained in adding a new depth, meaning and significance to astrology? We would be really intrigued to have comments from any astrology students out there do more research into this.

The Polarity displayed by the Hexagram is best viewed when the Hexagram is overlaid on the Tree of Life. In fact, we have described in some detail the three types of polarity observed in the Hexagram as well as what we call the Three Cycles (which equate to the three Alchemical Principles of Salt, Mercury, and Sulphur! among other groups of three) as well as the Fire and the Water triangles that, interlaced, form the hexagram.

The three polarities observed in the Hexagram also equate to three of the Laws or Principles that the Kybalion by the Three Initiates discusses: Vibration, Polarity and Rhythm. Vibration is in fact what we term 'vertical polarity'. Polarity is what we term 'horizontal polarity'. Rhythm is what we call 'active polarity'.

According to the Kybalion, '*Vibration is the great Third Hermetic Principle--the Principle of Vibration--embodies the truth that Motion is manifest in everything in the Universe--that nothing is at rest--that everything moves, vibrates, and circles. This Hermetic Principle was recognized by some of the early Greek philosophers who embodied it in their systems. But then, for centuries it was lost sight of by the thinkers outside of the Hermetic ranks. But in the Nineteenth Century physical science re-discovered the truth and the Twentieth Century scientific discoveries have added additional proof of the correctness and truth of this centuries-old Hermetic doctrine.*

*The Hermetic Teachings are that not only is everything in constant movement and vibration, but that the "differences" between the various manifestations of the universal power are due entirely to the varying rate and mode of vibrations. Not only this, but that even THE ALL, in itself, manifests a constant vibration of such an infinite degree of intensity and rapid motion that it may be practically considered as at rest, the teachers directing the attention of the students to the fact that even on the physical plane a rapidly moving object (such as a revolving wheel) seems to be at rest. The Teachings are to the effect that Spirit is at one end of the Pole of Vibration, the other Pole being certain extremely gross forms of Matter. Between these two poles are millions upon millions of different rates and modes of vibration.'*

In this book, we have discussed vertical polarity as that from spirit to matter, or perhaps from spiritual to physical. In fact, if a horizontal line is drawn on the hexagram at its mid-point, it becomes the above and the below. The spiritual above is mirrored by the physical below. Vertical polarity is like the way of creation.

Horizontal polarity is described in the Kybalion like this - "*Everything is dual; everything has poles; everything has its pair of opposites; like and unlike are the same; opposites are identical in nature, but different in degree; extremes meet; all truths are but half-*

*truths; all paradoxes may be reconciled."* In our book, we see horizontal polarity in the same way with two polar points reconciled at a third point through the Law of the Triangle.

We also talk about Active polarity - seen as the third dimensional polarity. It is the hardest to visualize and understand because it can only be observed when we look in three dimensions - it is depth, and we describe it as action - inaction. The Kybalion may just hint at this in the concept of Rhythm though Rhythm is described more as the pendulum swing between the two ends of horizontal polarity or pairs of opposites if you wish. But it is possible to see that Rhythm could equally well describe the cycle of action and inaction, rest, and motion that our third polarity suggests.

# Exercises

The exercises outlined in this book are meant to help both reinforce the concepts outlined in it as well as to guide you in a voyage of inner discover regarding the hexagram. However, to be effective they must be followed somewhat rigorously, and we strongly recommend that you note your reflections, thoughts, and realizations down in a well-structured magical diary. Include as you do so not just the daily exercises but also any other realizations that you might have during the day and any dreams that you recall during your study of the hexagram.

The exercises are designed to take a week each of six daily meditations with a rest day on the seventh day of the week. Each meditation session should last between 15 and 45 minutes. You may commence meditation with whatever opening sequence you are familiar with, but you should absolutely invoke the Kabbalistic Cross prior to beginning each daily exercise (Appendix 2)

Depending on the results obtained, readers may wish to repeat each week's mediations several times before moving onto the next set of exercises. Repetition of each set of exercises up to four times may be useful in reinforcing the concepts and providing layers of insights and realizations. This is entirely up to the individual.

These exercises are now also available as part of an online course that uses the materials from this book supplemented with video and other textual lessons to take you through the meditations and instruction. If interested, please do visit the school online at https://earth-magic-brno.teachable.com/ and sign up.

## What You Will Need

You will require a place where you can meditate uninterrupted to complete these exercises. If you have a temple use that and if not, then select a room where you can enjoy some solitude and quiet. Consider burning some incense or playing some relaxing music in the background. Have a pen and paper to hand to note down your impressions.

Additionally, you will need two large sheets of tracing paper, a ruler and a black felt tip pen. Some glue might be handy too!

There is no right or wrong way to approach meditation. There are no required positions, just that you be comfortable, supported, and able to relax deeply – and yet stay awake. Breathe deeply; allow all areas of your body to relax, letting go of tension in muscle and mind.

Hold the image or seed thought in your mind and follow where it leads, taking note of the ideas and impressions that arise to note down in your diary.

Above all, remember there is no wrong or right answer. This journey will be unique for every one of us.

# The Hexagram and the Elements

### Week One: Fire is the First born

*Day One:*

Before commencing the meditation session, draw a triangle with its single point upwards on a large piece of tracing paper. Study your drawing and then place the triangle you have drawn into memory so that you can easily visualise the triangle that represents the element of Fire.

Meditate on and visualise this symbol as clearly as you possibly can, holding the image firmly in the mind's eye, while reflecting on the nature of elemental Fire as both hot and expansive. Think of some of the qualities discussed earlier in this book. Try to contemplate and connect with the polar characteristics of Fire.

*Day Two:*

Meditate further on these polar characteristics of elemental Fire. Try to find as many examples as possible of these opposites and having done so, visualise them in action. After your meditation session, write the opposites down on the two basal points of your Fire triangle diagram where you think that they belong.

*Day Three:*

Meditate on how the opposite qualities of Fire that you came up with yesterday can be reconciled. Explore the single third upper point of the Fire triangle – what is it? What does it represent? What happens when you think of reconciling the pairs of opposites you have thought of? Write down anything that you come up with on your Fire triangle diagram.

*Day Four:*

Visualise your Fire triangle again and try to keep in mind the ideas and realisations that you have come up with so far and written on your diagram. The idea is to try to hold the triangle in mind, including the ideas on opposite qualities of Fire and how these opposites may be reconciled. Try not to visualise the triangle as it is on the paper with notes scribbled around it, but as a whole and complete symbol with the ideas of polarity inherent within it. Record any additional realisations as well as how this makes you feel.

*Day Five:*

Today, you will build a mental picture of an actual fire. Imagine the flames licking upwards in multiple colours, feel the heat of the fire on your skin, smell the acrid smell of the smoke from the fire and try to hear the fuel burning, crackling, and spitting. See the fire. Picture it clearly. See the action of its burning.

Use any aid to this visualisation that you can. For example, recall memories of a beach bonfire or Guy Faulk's night bonfire that you experienced as a child. Call up the smell of wood smoke. Feel the heat on the side of your body that is turned towards the flames; watch the pictures forming in the embers of red and gold, and note the blackened, silvered timbers as they burn. Be childlike in your exploration of this image, and the sounds and smell of fire. Enjoy the Fire and be totally absorbed by it.

*Day Six:*

Rebuild your mental picture of Fire as you did yesterday. Feel it, smell it,....and then go one step further. Now, become the Fire. *Be* fire. Burn as a flame rising upwards. Dance and flicker, become all the qualities of pure flame. Become the flames, become the fire. Imagine what it is like to be a Fire. What emotions do you feel? What sensations?

Record your feelings, insights, and experience in as much detail as you are able.

*Day Seven:*

Rest.

## Week Two: Water Flowing Freely

*Day One:*

Prior to meditation draw a triangle with its single point downwards on a second large piece of tracing paper. Place the triangle you have drawn into memory so that you can easily visualise the triangle representing Water.

Consider the nature of elemental Water as cold and contractive in your meditation. Consider the opposite qualities of water and record anything you come up with afterwards on your diagram in its appropriate place.

*Day Two:*

Meditate further on the polarities of elemental Water. Now try to find examples of these opposite qualities and visualise them in action. Write them down on the two basal points of your drawn Water triangle as you feel is appropriate.

*Day Three:*

Meditate on how the polarities that you came up with yesterday can be reconciled. Explore the single third point of the Water triangle – what is it? What does it represent? Think back to the examples given earlier in the book. What watery opposites come to your mind and how are they resolved?

Write down anything that you come up with on your Water triangle diagram.

*Day Four:*

Visualise the Water triangle and try to keep in mind the ideas and realizations that you have come up with so far and written on your diagram. The idea is to try to hold the triangle in mind including the ideas on polarities and their reconciliation. What does the polarity implicit in the element water represent? How are the polarities reconciled at that third upper point?

*Day Five:*

Build a mental picture of water. Imagine its coldness, wetness, and transparency. See the water flowing as a stream or a river, moving deep and slow, or chattering over stones. Hear its sounds and smell the freshness of the water. Feel it on your skin, taste it. Think of the ocean, rain, and other forms of water. Use any images you can to aid your visualisation such as waterfalls, ponds, lakes or running water. Call up images from your memory of the way you have known water. Let your emotions flow with the images.

Record all your feelings, insights, and thoughts.

*Day Six:*

Build your mental picture of Water as you did yesterday. Feel it, smell it, hear it….and then become it. Be water, flow like water in a stream. Imagine what it is like to be the element water. Imagine the movement; imagine where you have come from and where you are flowing. Imagine the life within, encompassed by water.

Record all your perceptions, feelings, and insights.

*Day Seven:*

Rest.

## Week Three: The Hexagram

*Day One:*

Take your two diagrams of the fire and water triangles and overlay them to form a hexagram. Study this symbol carefully and commit it to memory. Notice how the two triangles combine to form the hexagram and notice too how all four elemental triangles are represented in the hexagram. Meditate with a visual image of the hexagram in your mind's eye. Consider its shape, geometry, and symmetry as you do so and then record any realisations from the session.

*Day Two:*

Begin by visualising the hexagram as a symbol using your combined diagrams if necessary. Close your eyes. Hold the hexagram form in your mind and reflect on it as a symbol. Count and consider the six points and reflect on what they might represent and finally notice that there is a seventh, invisible point at the center of the hexagram. Reflect on this hidden seventh point. What does it represent?

Record your feelings, thoughts, and realisations.

*Days Three, Four and Five:*

Take your hexagram drawing and using a ruler, draw the horizontal and vertical axes of symmetry to form a superimposed equal armed cross. Then, again visualise the hexagram in your mind's eye. Try to rotate it and observe it in three dimensions – from all aspects. If you have difficulty with adding the extra dimensions, find an illustration of a Merkabah symbol to act as a reference point. What does this symbol mean for you? Think of the reconciliation of the opposites inherent in the form. Consider how each part of the hexagram is reflected perfectly across the axes of symmetry and reflect on the meaning of 'As above, so below' as demonstrated by this form.

Record what you see, think, and feel in your diary, remembering to add any realisations that come to you through the rest of the day.

*Day Six:*

Consider the occult maxim 'As above, so below' in the context of the hexagram and the realisations that you have had.

Record everything that you can on the diagram and in your diary.

*Day Seven:*

Rest.

## *Week Four: The Inner Child*

*Days One to Four:*

Again, visualise the hexagram but this time consider the polarities implicit in the hexagram itself. Consider what these polarities are, what they represent and how they are reconciled in the hidden seventh point of harmony. Think about the horizontal polarity, vertical polarity and even the in-out polarity (in the third dimension) and reflect on what they might represent and how *they* are reconciled.

Record your thoughts in your diary.

*Day Five:*

Today, using the realisations you had in the first four days of exercises, consider the seventh point – the point of harmony and balance. What does this point represent? What images does it provide you? What does it tell you about your own nature? What occult secret is it trying to suggest to you?

Carefully record all realisations.

*Day Six:*

Consider again the seventh point. Meditate on the idea that the seventh point is the hidden inner child of the sum of polarities in the triangles and the hexagram. Try to be that seventh point – imagine the peace and tranquillity of that seventh point – make it a place of sanctuary that you might wish to revisit in some future meditation.

Find that kernel of peace that is, as it were, at the eye of the storm. Find it within yourself and find yourself within It. Be there in that place of harmony, peace, and timelessness.

Make careful note of what you experience, think, and feel.

*Day Seven:*

Rest

## Week 5 – The Garden of Remembrance

### Day One through Three

Sit quietly and imagine yourself in a beautiful location. Feel yourself to be there. Try not to observe yourself but be part of it. You are sitting under a flowing willow tree on sandy soil surrounded by the vibrancy of nature. You can feel the rough bark of the tree behind your back. You see your feet stretched out before you.

Behind you is a forest, green and dense. In front of you is a beach of sand dunes, leading down to the ocean. You can hear crickets and bees buzzing and there are birds singing in the trees. It is peaceful and quiet except for these natural sounds and the faint sound of breakers on the beach.

The sun shines above you and you can feel its warmth even under the flowing branches of the willow. All is well and this place – this Garden of Remembrance – is yours and yours only. Picture this place as intently as you are able. Keep the images consistent from day to day while building in the details. Feel relaxed, peaceful, and happy.

### Days Four and Five

Imagine yourself in the usual spot under the willow. Feel at peace, building the scene around you. This is your place.

When you are ready and the visualisation is complete and steady, notice that there is a fire, a pyramidal blaze, on the beach in front of you. You can feel the heat from the flames, see the embers burning black and gold, hear the crackle and spitting of the fire and smell the wood smoke in your nostrils.

When you are ready, stare into the fire intently and imagine that the wood on the fire is all the things about you that need to be discarded and burned. Throw on the fire things like hatred and jealousy, misplaced desires and emotions as logs or fuel and let that fire burn, fuelled by these characteristics. It is not unpleasant to rid yourself of these things, carried so long like a burden of kindling on your back. It is a relief and a release to let go of them, watching them be consumed in the clean flame. Watch the changing, dancing colours of the flame as they are consumed and transformed.

Understand and know that as you throw each on the fire it is being transformed into the four elements – fire, water, air, and earth – in the form of flame and heat, water vapour and smoke, hot air and ash.

Take a special note of your feelings and thoughts as you go through this meditation.

*Day Six*

Repeat the previous exercise, but as you fuel the fire with unwanted attributes of yourself, become *yourself* the fire. Be the flames and the heat and rise slowly as a quivering flame. Float as heat, shimmering and shifting. Be the fire. You are the flame that burns and consumes, you are the fire of transformation.

Know that this fire burns inside of you eternally.

Write down your experience and emotions, and any realisations that come to you.

*Day seven*

Rest

## Week Six – The Circle of Healing

### Days One to Three

Again, build up in your mind's eye the Garden of Remembrance and see the fire burning steadily on the beach before you.

Once again, fuel the fire with your unwanted emotions and characteristics and see it burn strongly and brightly. Shift your consciousness and become the fire. Feel yourself as flame, transforming the fuel beneath. Burn brightly and rise imagining yourself at first a flickering flame and then as the hot air that rises up and up. Float there as heat, suspended above the flame.

Write down your feelings, what you think of and the realisations you have throughout the day.

### Days Four to Six

Carefully build up the scene and repeat the previous exercise. Become the flame, become the heat, and rise above the fire. But this time, continue to rise and up and up until you find yourself in another place, high up above the Garden of Remembrance.

Know that you are now in a most holy place and be reverent and respectful.

You will observe that you now sit inside a circle of standing stones. There are six standing stones equally spaced in a circle and you sit in the very center. The ground is warm beneath you; a cool breeze touches your cheek.

The stone circle is on top of a wide, flat-topped mountain and so you can see little but clear blue sky beyond the standing stones. Above you, directly above you, is a large golden Sun. It does not move. It is always directly above you.

Nestled on the ground before you is a wide golden bowl containing fresh water. You will wash your face, your hands, and your feet in this bowl of water as you should in a holy place, carefully and with reverence, feeling the pure touch of the water on your skin.

You can feel the energy here. It is a healing energy, and you instinctively understand that here, as you sit in contemplative silence, you are being healed. You know that your symbolic act of washing is now working in your body, spirit, and soul. The holy water is cleansing, washing, and quenching.

Sit for as long as you desire and feel the healing process at work and know that this is the action of the sacred water with which you washed.

*Day Seven*

Rest as usual.

## Week Seven – The Hexagram and Tree of Life

*Day One:*

Draw a picture of the Tree of Life and use a red and blue pen to draw the two triangles of the hexagram on the Tree. Red for Fire and Blue for Water. Research and label each point/Sephirah and Path from the Tree of Life included in the hexagram and study the correspondences carefully. Write these down on your diagram adding as much detail as you can.

Repeat your visit to the Circle of Healing starting in the Garden of Remembrance. Build the fire, feed it, become the fire, rise as flame and heat, and then ritually wash in the Circle of Healing. From now on, you will do this each day wherever it says, 'Visit the Circle of Healing'. In the Circle of Healing, continue to consider the Hexagram, its points, pathways, and symmetry.

Note your thoughts, feelings, and inspirations.

*Day Two:*

Focus on the Fire triangle and simply meditate and study in meditation the linkage between the points of Fire triangle and the Sephirah on the Tree.

Repeat your visit to the Circle of Healing. In the Circle of Healing, continue to consider the Hexagram, its points, pathways, and symmetry.

Note what you experience and learn from this.

*Day Three:*

Focus on the water triangle and simply mediate and study the linkages between the points of the Water triangle and the Sephirah on the tree.

Again, then visit the Circle of Healing and note down your experiences and thoughts. In the Circle of Healing, continue to consider the Hexagram, its points, pathways, and symmetry.

*Days Four to Six:*

Now focus on the total Hexagram and all the linkages on the Tree of Life. Contemplate the three polarities on the tree and reflect on how this corresponds to your own make up and psyche.

Before finishing visit the Circle of Healing.

As always, note your experiences.

*Day Seven*

Rest as usual.

## *Week Eight – The Planets and Metals*

*Day One:*

Take your Hexagram diagram on the Tree and add in the attributions for the metals and planets. Do a bit of your own research in terms of the meanings attributed to the planets and the metals and write them too on the diagram. Your own insights are always the most relevant to you.

After this please visit the Circle of Healing.

*Days Two to Six:*

Visit the Circle of Healing. While there, contemplate the whole picture of the Hexagram, sephiroth, metals and planets. Visualise the diagram you drew in your mind and let it permeate your soul.

As always, note down everything you experience.

*Day Seven:*

rest

## Week Nine – The Cycles

*Day One:*

Identify and familiarize yourself with the three cycles on your diagram and write in any additional notes and explanations you desire to place there.

Visit the Circle of Healing.

Record your meditation.

*Days Two to Six:*

Visit the Circle of Healing and contemplate there the three cycles and what they mean. Think about the correspondences and think about the three alchemical principles represented by these. Consider the polarity aspects of the cycles. The best approach will be to take one of the three cycles each day and on the last two days try to work through all three together.

Note down your thoughts and feelings.

## Week Ten– The Great Work

*Day One:*

Visit the Circle of Healing. Build up the picture in your imagination carefully. Sit there in a meditation within a meditation and see a single timeless and eternal point of Light.

Consider this point and then see a flash of Light – the flash of creation – and watch as a concentric circle of energy ripples out from that point.

See six points equally spaced on the concentric circle as it expands, forming a hexagram enclosed within the circle.

Record your meditation.

*Day Two:*

Repeat all aspects of Day One but now contemplate deeply the seven points – the central point surrounded by the six. Think about this as representative of the macrocosm and of yourself as microcosm.

What does this tell you?

Write down your thoughts.

*Days Three to Six:*

Repeat Day Two but before returning to normal waking consciousness, see the circle collapse back into the single point, like a vast wave of Light flowing back upon itself. Observe that single eternal point once more. Consider the idea that this point contains all the others – all their correspondences and characteristics. Realise that the All is contained within the One, and the One is in All.

What does this mean to you?

Write down your reflections and realisations.

*Day Seven:*

Rest

## Next Steps

After completion of this set of exercises, the reader may desire to continue with the Garden of remembrance and Circle of Healing meditations and add their own meditations when in the Circle of Healing. We believe that these exercises will form the basis for a lot more work on the Hexagram and perhaps realisations about the Great work. We would love to hear from you so please feel free to write to us at garymvasey@gmail.com with any thoughts or comments that you may have.

# PostScript and Dedication

This book is dedicated to my good friend and co-author Sue C. Vincent who passed away a year or so ago. Her joy of life, the ability to constantly see the good in everyone and sense of fun, is missed on a daily basis...... Hoping you are plying out wherever you are Sue. Her take on the Qabbalah – included as Appendix 1 – is a work of beauty.

# References

**Bardon, Franz**, Initiation into Hermetics, Merkur Publishing, 2007

**deMontfaucon de Villars, Abbe N.**, Comte de Gabalis, Kessinger Publishing Company

**Vasey, G. Michael**, Inner Journeys: Explorations of the Soul, Thoth, 2006

# Appendix 1

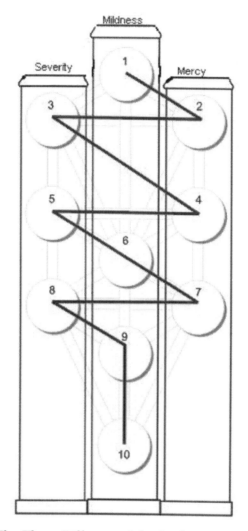

*The Three Pillars and the Lightning Flash*

## *An Overview of the Tree of Life*

The Tree of Life is a familiar symbol today to anyone with an interest in esoteric thought and there are thousands of books available about the Qabalah. Interpretations may vary, but one thing they all have in common, it seems, is the general acceptance that the Tree, as used in the Western Mystery Tradition, is a living, growing system, best understood by experience.

As it now stands, there is a wide gulf between the origins of the Tree and its practical application in the Mysteries. Our own scholarship leaves much to be desired, but we have lived and worked with the Tree for decades, and it runs closely through all that we do.

Although this book will appeal primarily to those who are already familiar with the symbolism of the Tree of Life, in this appendix we would like to share with you the basic meaning of the glyph of the Tree as it is used in modern Mystery Schools for those less familiar with this system. As with most things, the more you can contribute to the exercises in terms of knowledge and understanding, the more you will get out of them.

Remember that the Tree is a glyph, a representation, and an attempt to capture in a single symbol a series of abstract concepts and as such it works very well. From the esoteric viewpoint it has been likened to a cosmic filing system where all knowledge, all belief systems and mythologies can be placed, studied, and understood in their relationships to each other and to the Divine Life.

Continuous meditation and study by students the world over, through hundreds of years, have built up an accessibility with this glyph that allows the student to 'tune in' to the ideas and archetypes of the Tree without the need for a lifetime's study… though there is so much to be learned from it that it would repay several lifetime's worth of serious study and still throw up some surprises.

The Tree of Life represents the journey of the forces of Creation and the cycle of life. Look at the picture of the Tree (Figure 6). There are 10 spheres, called Sephiroth. The 22 Paths connect these. The Sephiroth and the lines between them make up the 32 Paths of the Tree of Life. The Sephiroth are arranged in three columns that represent the pillars of the Temple.

There is also an 11th sphere, usually represented by a dotted circle, which is the Invisible Sephirah, Daath, situated on the Middle Pillar between the first and sixth spheres. We will deal with this Sephirah separately.

Behind the first Sephirah, Kether, are drawn the three Veils of Negative existence. These are represented as half circles and are called Ain, Negativity, Ain Soph, the Limitless, and Ain Soph Aur, the Limitless Light. These Veils are, at the simplest level, merely a device that recognises the limitations of the perceptions of mankind at this present moment of evolution. In other words, the Veils are the point at which we say our understanding can go no further. What is beyond the Veils is the state of potential Being that surpasses anything we can currently understand, surmise of conjecture. It is the place beyond the origin of God.

The Veils can, perhaps be said to be both fixed and moveable. Fixed, because they mark the boundary of understanding, moveable as we are constantly evolving and as we do so our understanding itself expands. However, for practical purposes they work very well to define a horizon beyond which we cannot yet see.

The Three Pillars are the Pillars of the Temple. On the right is the silver Pillar of Mercy, called Jachin. It is headed by Chokmah and represents Force. The black Pillar of Severity on the left is called Boaz, and, headed by Binah, represents Form. The central Pillar of Mildness is the Pillar of Equilibrium, perfect balance.

The path of the Lightning Flash shows the descent of Power from the Source in Kether, to manifestation in Malkuth. This is termed 'involution'. The return part of the circuit, from Malkuth to Kether, is evolution. Each of the Sephiroth equates to a state of Being, or Becoming, stages in evolution.

Imagine the nature of Kether as a pure, undefined, unmanifest awareness. The First Swirlings. An abstract sentience, pure 'Beingness'. Imagine that this awareness becomes aware of Itself. The pressure builds and the awareness overflows, becoming Chokmah, a mirror image of Kether. This movement in the First Swirlings is dynamic, the first potency of the potential. In turn, Chokmah overflows and forms Binah, where the first possibilities of Form begin. Together they form the first Trinity, the Supernal Triangle.

From Binah via Daath, emanates Chesed, where the first constraints are imposed on the abstract Form as natural law, organisation begins. Chesed gives rise to Geburah, where the rules of Chesed are imposed as the discipline of the idea of Form.

Tiphareth, on the Middle Pillar, is the heart or Christ centre, a place of synthesis and the perfect balance of Form and Force. These three form the second triangle and signify a 'gear change'.

Netzach arises from Tiphareth, where Force is organised by the dynamic feminine, balanced by Hod, where Form is ensouled by the forces of Nature. In Yesod Force and Form have 'crystallised' the astral proto- matter, until finally in Malkuth we have Manifestation.

Remember that the Sephiroth are not places, nor are they gods... they are states of becoming.

We will not give the Tables of Correspondences here; they are widely available these days. In practical terms, however, by assigning the gods and symbols, the archetypes, and angels, to the Sephiroth in accordance with the nature of the Force they express, we can begin to see the patterns of Life.

## *Kether, the Crown.*

Kether is the Crown... that which sits above the head, so imagine it as slightly removed from all that we know. It is the purest possibility of Becoming. Undifferentiated, a harmonious chaos of potency, arising in the sphere of Kether from the Great Unmanifest beyond the veils. It is nothing and everything, all that can and will be, all that has been. It is the merest possibility of matter and yet it is pure consciousness under pressure. All the potency of the Great Unmanifest pours in, as if through a pinhole in the blackness of space.

This is the Point within the circle, Macroprosopos, the Head which is Not. All these are images of Kether which help give the mind some spar to cling to in the unfamiliar waters of Becomingness.

The sphere of Kether sits at the head of the Middle Pillar, and when that glyph is visualised as superimposed on oneself, rests above the head. Its very presence is a constant reminder and symbol of our highest aspirations. It is a junction between the levels of our Self, being both the highest point of our lower self and the lowest point of our higher being. It is, therefore, both Kether and Malkuth and the potential of the one is seen in the qualities of the other. As always, 'as above so below', not different in anything except degree.

The sphere of Kether is a node of union and communication within us, permitting a two-way exchange between the levels of our being. Experience of material conditions and the lessons we (hopefully) learn can be transmuted and sent up the planes, while inner knowledge and inspiration can be sent through and crystallised into terms our denser selves can comprehend.

Conceive of all the spheres operating in a similar manner, with the Kether sphere being the area where transmission is refined and attuned, before traversing the veils to the next level.

On the Tree the sphere equates to the highest conceivable state of godhead, the fount of all force and form in its most ethereal state. The pure raw potential of beingness and becoming with all the pressure of the Unmanifest behind it.

Take the image of an hourglass. The top half of the hourglass stretches beyond the veils into the unimaginable unmanifest and the lower half reaches down the Tree towards the very concrete existence we know. The waist of this glass is Kether. The point on which all pressure is concentrated before the outflowing.

One can see the same effect through the other spheres of the middle pillar and on down through other Trees on other levels and can only assume that the hourglass effect carries on up the planes too, to extend beyond Kether to some infinite infinity.

## Chokmah – Wisdom

Go back to the image of the hourglass and see the pressure building. Imagine, if you will that the pressure is sentient and seeks to know itself. As the pressure reaches a critical point, fuelled by the desire to know, it overflows and emanates a mirror image of itself so that it may see itself. This mirror image is Chokmah, Wisdom. In knowing itself, the pure, abstract sentience of Kether gains the Wisdom to see itself as it is but reflected.

Chokmah is the second Sephirah and sits at the head of the Pillar of Mercy. It is the first emanation of Kether, the state where force first identifies itself. In Kether is the source, the purest, abstract potential. That pure potency overflows into the sphere of Chokmah to become the first state where force has an understandable direction. In Chokmah is the dynamic, positive potency of creation. Perhaps the existence of the Chokmah state serves to draw force from Kether. All the symbolism associated with Chokmah reinforces the idea, being phallic, which is the simplest symbolic expression of potent maleness.

This is not a sphere of sexuality in the mundane sense, but the driving force, the impetus behind the creative principle. One can see it as the desire for expression through creation, which cannot come into being until it has expressed itself by overflowing to form Binah. It is the paradox behind the myths of the masturbating gods who produced their children from their own bodies. Until Binah, the first negative sphere, comes into being, there can be no balanced duality and therefore no creation of functional form, even at this abstract level. Yet Binah emanates from Chokmah, so the creative force has, of necessity, expressed itself independently. However, as Chokmah receives itself from Kether, it is receptive and negative in relation to Kether and so duality, and the possibility of polarity, come into manifestation with Chokmah, although polarity cannot be expressed in function until Binah has come into being.

Chokmah is the Archetypal Father and equates to the Elder Gods of the various pantheons, the fathers of the gods. Although prayer, as taught at least by the Christian Church, should go via Tiphareth to Kether, perhaps Chokmah is as far as many can apprehend. Chokmah is the first sphere where we can begin to personalise the forces involved, albeit at an abstract level, in terms we can begin to grasp and relate to our own existence.

Chokmah represents the dynamism of the first outward movement of the Kether force. Where Kether is pure force, the First Swirlings, Chokmah is force with purpose.

Kether is pressurised possibility. It requires the existence of Chokmah to receive the outpouring of Its potential. Yet Chokmah requires that outpouring to exist, in the same way that Binah calls force from Chokmah yet owes its existence to Chokmah. There can be no existence without the need or desire to exist. Everything is linked in an unbroken chain; everything has its beginning in a preceding state and causes the becoming of the next state. So, all states of existence are implicit in Kether and, by extension, implicit in all states individually. It is the levels on which those forces operate that determine the way in which they manifest. Everything has its place within the universe, like a vast machine of interlinked cogs, each dependent upon the action of the previous cog to impel its own motion and responsible for the propulsion of the subsequent cog, in an endless translation of force, changing gear at every level and returning the amplified force to the beginning.

## Binah - Understanding

Binah stands at the head of the Pillar of Severity and is the third Sephirah. With Kether and Chokmah it forms the Supernal Triangle, the first Trinity, Potential, Force and Form. Together, these three are a balanced triad which create the conditions necessary to form a functional fourth. This is reflected all down the Tree and through life in general, where a particular state of being (or state of mind), backed by the desire to effect a change, produces an action which in turn results in an altered state. That resulting altered state is of another level than the original one, just as Daath is removed from the Tree. Each of the triads on the Tree results in a change of state. The same principle applies to the Kether, Tiphareth, Yesod trinity which crosses the barriers to give rise to the manifested life of Malkuth.

Binah is the great feminine principle behind creation. The sphere is negative, passive, and receptive, and in relation to the preceding Sephirah. It has, however, the dynamic force of creation behind it, and it is positive in relation to subsequent spheres. It is, perhaps, the vessel of dynamic force, rather than the initiator. This negative Sephirah is where the possibility of form is conceived. The symbolism associated with Binah reinforces this. Binah is the Great Sea, Marah, and life arose in the vast cauldron of the waters. It is also called the Great Mother and it is the mother's role to give form to the life within her. This is the great, dark womb of creation and as the womb is the gate of birth, it is also the gate of death as every birth carries its own death with it; birth and death being two facets of the same jewel.

It is in the silence of the Binah state that we ourselves brood ideas and concepts that will one day bear fruit, though the idea may have been born of the dynamism of Chokmah, inspired by the potential of Kether.

Binah sits at the head of the Pillar of Severity. This is the sphere where the concept of form is conceived, and form carries limits. On the one hand, this is a wonderful thing, for pure potential alone can never achieve, it needs to be organised into form before it can accomplish anything other than simply being. On the other hand, every form has its limitations. In dreams one can fly, but the physical body has no wings. The limitations of a particular form can only be transcended by changing gear and working at a higher level and accepting that the results may never be obviously visible. Form also has a limited shelf-life, decaying or degrading over time and this too contains the possibilities for anything constrained to work within its limits. Binah is the mother which broods, births and teaches. It is also the role of the mother to instil discipline. In general, although it is usually the father who enforces discipline, it is from our mothers we ingest most of the life-lessons we learn as we grow. In this sense also, it fits that Binah should head the Pillar of Severity. Discipline is inherent in form, as form requires organisation and relationships between the particles of its being.

## Daath – Knowledge

This sphere is known as the Invisible Sephirah and is not numbered or counted with the others.

On the Tree, Daath is shown on the Middle Pillar below Kether as the downward point of the triangle formed by Chokmah and Binah. It reflects Kether at a different level and that which reflects in turn into Tiphareth, parallel to Kether. The more one looks, the more one is struck by the reflections of the spheres and their resonance at different levels. The symmetry and rhythm of the Tree is beautiful: an atomic dance at cosmic level.

Daath is called the Sephirah of Knowledge. If Kether represents the potent pre-becoming of force, then Daath, the synthesis of the first three Sephiroth is perhaps the cohesive potency which organises the pure being of Kether and the duality of Chokmah and Binah into something approaching form. Is it perhaps the matrix of manifestation as we grasp it? Daath is of the Tree, but not on it, a state of being behind, but not a visible part, of the descent of force into form. Perhaps we can conceive of Daath as the vision of creation in the cosmic mind.

If Kether represents pure consciousness in the highest part of man, the point where perhaps the soul can reach out towards the Source, then perhaps Daath is the place within the soul where humanity has its conscience. Not the acquired moral conscience conditioned by religion, state, or circumstance, but the innate conscience of mankind. The 'guardian angel' that whispers in the racial ear, giving us knowledge of the rightness and order of life.

On a lower arc, it represents the abstract intellect as opposed to intelligence. Not the decision maker, but the power behind it.

One can see Daath as being out of sync somehow, though designedly so. One step removed in space and time from the immediate now though perhaps it is the impetus behind that now and the matrix in which it is held.

Daath spans the gulf between Being and Becoming. It is the gear change between abstract and concrete, yet itself fits neither category, having (despite mixed metaphor) a foot in both worlds. It is a mirror that reflects both ways inwards to infinity, up and down the planes. Like a lens it magnifies and concentrates, being the point of translation, a gateway, the state of being behind the organising principle.

Like the magnetic lines of force around a magnet, Daath draws in the raw materials of the cosmos and organises them like iron filings, held in intricate patterns. If Kether holds the potential, Daath holds the pattern. Daath is, perhaps, comparable to the spatial stresses between the protons, neutrons, and electrons of each atomic particle, both cause and effect of the gravitational pull of the movement of life. Each of the spheres is a two-way portal.

## Chesed – Mercy

Chesed, Mercy, is the fourth Sephirah (not counting Daath which sits at a level removed). It is the central sphere of the Pillar of Mercy and the first sphere after the Abyss. It is the first sphere to receive and take its nature from the balanced triad of Kether, Chokmah and Binah.

The Supernal triangle deals with the abstract principles behind existence, Chesed seems to refer to the first principles behind manifested life. The magical image presents the enthroned king, holding the orb and sceptre and crowned. It is an image of stability. The king is crowned, his kingship established; he is seated upon the throne, solid and square. The concept is one of established strength, order, and the rule of law. The sphere represents these principles at the root of life. The first triangle, now balanced and interacting to create the conditions necessary for the possibility of manifestation, overflow to give rise to Chesed. As the Abyss is crossed, the forces change gear and the abstract possibility becomes established 'reality' in a sense we can relate to, organised into natural, Universal Law.

Chesed sits at the centre of the Pillar of Mercy, its number is four and the square, a four-sided figure, is amongst its symbols. The square is a solid, balanced shape with perfect symmetry. It represents the building block of life, but it is a two-dimensional shape, as opposed to the cube associated with Tiphareth. This is not yet manifested life as we perceive it from our current perspective, but the controlling principle it is based upon. In Daath the balanced, purposeful potential of the Supernals changes frequency, as it were. In Chesed the forces have achieved that internal balance of stresses that allows them to organise into that state where the ordered progression into manifestation can begin. The regal image of the law-giving monarch, stately and composed on his throne illustrates this well. Jupiter is assigned to Chesed. The counterparts from other pantheons like Zeus and Amun are also the High Kings of the gods. Not the Elder Gods from the oldest tales, who would be assigned to Chokmah, but the fathers of Man, the great gods who rule humanity, often through the intermediary of the 'lesser' gods.

Chesed is the result of the functional balance achieved by the three Supernals. It gives form to their combined force, albeit tenuous in terms of our experience. It is the rock upon which manifested life stands and holds the germinating seeds of our being. Coming down the Pillar of Mercy, Chesed reflects the nature of Chokmah, but stepped down to a more reachable level. The gods of this sphere (despite some of the tales associated with them in mythology) are benign, paternal deities who love their creations in spite of their faults.

Chesed is not a sphere of details, but of concepts. The broad lines of manifestation may be determined by its influence, but the detail comes in later. Yet it is here is that human understanding can begin to comprehend at a human, rather than abstract, level. The state represented by Chesed is still far removed from our normal perception of reality but can be understood in its terms. The anthropomorphic images begin to take on a recognisable life, parallel to our own, whereas the images associated with the Supernals evoke an emotional response to godhead.

If the gods were 'created' by man to allow him to understand the aspects of his Creator in bite size pieces (and the Tree is a glyph which achieves the same thing in greater depth) then Chesed equates to the highest of the gods, we learned to love with a love akin to our own. Chokmah and Binah were the great Father and Mother we worshipped with loving awe, while Kether was the Great God behind the gods.

## Geburah – Strength, Severity

Geburah, Strength, Severity, also called Din, Justice and Pachad, Fear, is associated with Mars, which brings images of warfare. It sits below Binah on the Pillar of Severity and is traditionally the fifth Sephirah. However, the sphere of Chesed balances this sphere on the Tree. It holds no evil, but as the necessarily ruthless element in creation, it is that which discards the outmoded, fights for justice and cuts away the unnecessary.

It is easy to see how we, as human beings, accumulate clutter in our lives. Whether that be the overstuffed wardrobe of things that will never fit again, but to which we fondly cling, or the mental and emotional clutter which we accumulate and allow to cloud the clarity of our inner sight. Geburah, I think, is the black bag and sweeping brush of the Cosmos.

Equally, one can see Geburah in the idea of the natural evolution of the species, where many species that can no longer adapt are lost. Or in the evolution of thought, where ideas are lost in the mists of time, as they are replaced by new ideas that have been built on the back of their predecessors. One can imagine how scary the thought of a round world must have been, with people expecting to fall off, and we know how much of a furore the new ideas caused within the Church. Perhaps the acceptance of those new ideas, taking time to filter through the ranks, must have contained an element of Geburah working on autopilot, gently, behind the scenes. Where the changes are more radical, one can see the King in his chariot cutting through the bonds to release imprisoned minds.

Geburah seems to be all dynamism. It is probably the most 'active' of the Sephiroth in this sense. It is necessary force, quick justice, surgical excision. But it is also the strong, protective sword arm. It is easy to give in to inertia. Geburah is the well-placed kick that wakes us up again. It is easy to founder among the humdrum needs and tasks of living. Geburah is the staircase to the clean air above where the view is clear. Many do not like the feel of this sphere. But it inspires respect.

Geburah is the opposing stress that balances the Mercy of Chesed. Justice, when it is served, is seldom easy or pleasant, but is needful. Severity, strict discipline, and order are also necessary.

The second triad on the Tree is that of Chesed, Geburah and Tiphareth. That is Mercy, Severity and Beauty. Mercy that is not weakness, Severity that is needful, because of the Beauty that is the Love that balances all. All that has been before and all that is yet to come is held in the poised equilibrium, the perfect balance that is Tiphareth. These are all qualities that we, as human beings, can relate to and translate into terms of everyday living, and one feels that with this Triangle begins the formation of personal consciousness at a level that is at once removed from our normal human consciousness and yet which provides the first organisation of consciousness at individual level. It has been called the Moral or Ethical Triangle, and it is largely our morals or ethics that define who we are as individuals.

## Tiphareth - Beauty

Tiphareth is the central sphere of the Tree, the point where worlds meet. It is the heart of the Tree, all the emanations from the other spheres flow directly into and out of Tiphareth, save only Malkuth, which has access only via the mediating influence of Yesod.

It is the balancing point of the Tree; all the spheres touch it and are touched by it equally. In Tiphareth is found the centre of equilibrium for all the spheres.

From above, Kether is reflected; from below, Yesod, with Malkuth completing the circuit. Force and form perfectly poised. It is this sphere that forms the centre of the Mystical Hexagram.

It is this harmony that renders the sphere more comprehensible and attainable. The gods assigned to Tiphareth are the 'human' gods, those whose stories we tell our children and whom we love. Not the great and mysterious God of all, so far removed from our understanding that we can only worship in awe, but the Light-bearers who carried fire from heaven so we could learn to see.

Tiphareth is the rainbow bridge between the upper and lower

realms of the Tree. It is the link between force and form. It is the point on the Middle Pillar to which normal human understanding can reach before it must transcend logic.

From Kether it is the state where force has coalesced to a comprehendible form, crystallised from the interaction of Gedulah (Chesed) and Geburah. From Malkuth it symbolises the return.

It is the sun centre, and like the sun, its force rays out from the centre. The sun gods are assigned to this sphere, the givers of Light and life.

The sacrificed gods are also attributed to Tiphareth. Christ, the Divine Son, was the mediator between God the Father and mankind and gave his life for the redemption of man, according to the teachings of the Christian Church. 'No man cometh unto the Father but by me'. Kether can only be reached through Tiphareth and the change of state the sphere represents.

Osiris, too, was a teacher of man, sacrificed and resurrected as the green god of rebirth. I think Tiphareth represents the rebirth of the soul to a higher state.

In many magical systems the sphere or state of being of Tiphareth represents what they called "Knowledge and conversation of the Holy Guardian Angel." This is complete connection and union with the Higher Self.

Kether is the Father and Tiphareth the Son, the Child. A child reflects the parent on a 'lesser' scale, retaining genetic traits directly attributable to the parent whilst adding those of its own, conditioned, and influenced by its origins. A child can learn from the parent, assimilating the knowledge of the parent and using it as the thrust block for its own growth and evolution, potentially surpassing the parent as it grows. Through Tiphareth, the force which had its origins in Kether is returned to its source, refined, expanded, and enriched.

Tiphareth is Kether on a lower arc.

Yet Tiphareth is also the King, reigning over the lower levels and giving order.

The similarities between the Qabalistic symbolism and that of Christianity are self-evident and explain much that the Bible offers. The Osirian myth also is clarified when considered on the Tree as the death and rebirth signify the passage to wider life through the transition of Tiphareth.

Tiphareth is sacrifice and redemption. From the Cosmic levels, Force sacrifices its freedom and binds itself into Form. From the material plane, it is the level where Force loosens its bonds. It does not need to be one of a pair of Sephirah as it contains its own opposing stresses in perfect balance. It is Harmony. It is poised between the Manifest and Unmanifest, and is the conduit through

which all life passes on the outward and inward journey.

In many systems the Sephiroth of the Middle Pillar correspond to the major initiations while those of the outer pillars represent the paths towards those initiations where knowledge and understanding is acquired and assimilated, bringing those aspects into harmony within each soul prior to the rite of passage.

## *Netzach – Victory*

Netzach, Victory, is the sphere assigned to Venus. Venus/Aphrodite was commonly portrayed as the goddess of love. Beautiful, exotic, sensual. Botticelli represents her as foam born, carried on the crest of the waves in the shell, a fertility symbol. She is not, however, perceived as a fertility goddess, but rather as the force behind fertility. The instigator of the desire that calls up the creative force in man and God. She portrays womankind as dynamic, the initiator, rather than the vessel of birth and death. She represents the awakening of force at instinctive level.

All the symbols assigned to this sphere resound with overtones of sensuality. Yet this is a Holy Sephirah, and there is nothing base about this. This is the pure impulsion of instinct, the response to divine force. Victory indeed!

If Netzach is the sphere of the instinctive idea, the non-concrete concept that eventually causes action, then it is a dynamic sphere, placed upon the Pillar of mercy. It seems very feminine in its symbolism to be on this pillar, but the intuitive leap of ideas is also a feminine trait. Do the minds of women function most naturally in

Netzach? Are the more logical minds of men more naturally suited to the climate of Hod? And as we walk the Paths of the Tree, we must learn to function equally well in both!

Going back to the symbolism of Venus, this pair of Hod and Netzach is about a more tangible polarity. Netzach calls forth the creative forces from above and below, conceiving the shape of things to come. Hod, reflecting Chesed, gathers these concepts and organises them into form. This is reflected in the material earth by the act of sex itself. The foreplay and lovemaking are a calling forth. It produces nothing but the idea of, and desire for, satisfaction. Pleasure and anticipation are physical manifestations of that idea. But, when that idea is realised, it calls forth the sperm that is the seed of new life.

Netzach reflects the sphere of Geburah, a dynamic, drastic, sphere, but tempered by the transmutation of Tiphareth. Mars and Venus with Love in between. It is perhaps, easiest to see with this pair, how the opposing pillars reflect within themselves the other spheres.

One can see Netzach as relating to the intuitive emotions, the leaps of faith, the artistic vision in man. All these things are part of us, yet also still removed from a tangible reality. They are concepts we can understand and feel, but not measure and quantify. Netzach is the impetus behind manifestation, but of itself, is not yet manifest. It is a force of nature, a divine force on one level, a basic instinct on another.

## Hod - Glory

Hod sits on the Pillar of Severity, below Geburah and opposite Netzach. The magical image is that of a hermaphrodite, a being neither male nor female, but containing elements of both. I conceive of this image as something which is in perfect balance, like the soul should be, without the need for differentiation. I also conceive of it as being pure, completed potential yet not quite manifest. Hod holds everything in readiness. On the inward arc, all forms can be expressed through the medium of Hod, which holds the possibility of everything. On the return it is perhaps the point at which form, and force begin to separate out, like blood in a centrifuge.

I see Hod as a vessel for the forms we create. This is not yet solid earth, but the place where form is brought to life from the mind of creation. This is, perhaps where the artist first' sees' the image he conceived in Netzach. It is subtle and tenuous, but reachable. It can be gathered and brought down into manifestation, translated by a paintbrush or pen. It does not yet exist, but the blueprint has been drawn up.

It follows that the forms we build in visualisation are also imprinted on the tenuous almost-matter of Hod. Not formed but designed already. Yesod is the sphere where we can reach the images, but Hod is where the images are formed, born of the concepts of Netzach.

If Yesod is the sphere where subtle forms become tangible and Netzach where the emotional/instinctive concept is conceived, then Hod is the design studio that assembles all the pre-production elements. The form in Hod is a prototype, where it can be examined from all angles before the force is allowed in from above and before it is allowed to manifest below. It is a proving ground for form.

It is also the sphere associated with magic and this would make sense, as the magician is working with generally astral forms, that must begin as an idea, and yet also, once 'designed', need to be animated by the very real forces of creation to function. Ensouling a thought form, must be done in this sphere of working, by drawing down force from above to complete the form before it becomes 'concrete' in the astral realm.

One may see this third triad as the 'factory' of manifestation. Where all the elements needed from idea to production are brought together. More than any other triad, it is difficult to separate the three, and one keeps referring to the others to elucidate each one. This is the earthiest of the triangles, yet still one step away from manifestation. It is still finer than Malkuth. Perhaps it is this proximity to the earth we know that makes it more difficult to define, because the similarities are glaring, but at the same time, the gap so wide.

Very human emotions can be understood in terms of these three, and this seems to be a necessity. Perhaps to find this triangle within oneself and balance it as it is on the Tree would be the single, most useful thing we could do for our mental and emotional health.

Victory, Glory, and Foundation. It is a triumphant liturgy on which to base manifestation and shouts out loud the holiness of life.

There are many patterns on the Tree. The first ones are obvious. There are the three pillars, the three Triangles, there are the paths that connect, turning a cosmic glyph to something that resembles a molecular diagram... Molecules, held together by the stresses to form a building block. And this is also true of the Tree, perhaps, for there is tree after Tree as one looks, inherent in life as within each sphere, extending inwards and outwards to an unknowable infinity. It is a dizzying concept to try and hold long enough to examine. One could, perhaps, find any pattern one looked for on the Tree reflected in life.

## Yesod – Foundation

Yesod is called the Foundation. If Daath is the matrix which holds the basis of becoming, then Yesod is the matrix which holds the basis of matter. (It is an easier concept to visualise than to describe accurately!) All the spheres pour their essence directly into Yesod, save only Kether and Daath, which must pass through Tiphareth. It holds all the potential of Kether, but on a lower arc. Yesod is the organising principle behind the life we know. The god name is

Shaddai el Chai, the Almighty Living God. The name suggests a level of manifestation we can approach and begin to understand. Yet a god, by definition, is not of the same level of creation as we mere mortals and the form of Yesod is still one step removed from matter as we generally understand it to be.

Yesod is the Foundation of life, but not yet the manifested life we know. It is the root which feeds life, drawing sustenance from all that has gone before. The spheres of the Middle Pillar are like transformers in the evolutionary current, where the forces are stepped up or down, according to whether they are on the evolutionary or involutionary arc. Yesod fine tunes the emanations of the preceding spheres to allow the diversification into form.

Each of the spheres of the Middle Pillar marks a change of state. The forces are the same from Kether to Malkuth, but they present a different aspect at each level. The spheres equate to the changes in consciousness of the cosmic forces and equally to the changes as consciousness rises in Man.

Each sphere is both a repository and transmitter of forces. There is the still, calm centre where the forces of each sphere are in balance and one can begin to touch the essence of that particular sphere, a 'place' where the inpouring and outpouring forces are poised in balance. A harmonious core, but not passive. There is also the dual face of each Sephirah, for each one is at the same time receiving the influx of force from both the preceding and subsequent spheres, on both the inward and outward arcs, and transmuting those forces before they continue their journey. Each of the Sephiroth, therefore, is both dynamic and passive, positive and negative in relation to those around it. Also, each would therefore also be positive or negative in relation to whether it was being 'viewed' from Kether or Malkuth, from the perspective of evolution or involution.


## Malkuth – the Kingdom

Malkuth is at the base of the Middle Pillar. We picture it beneath our foot, which seems right, as Malkuth is the starting point of our return to the Light, the thrust block of spiritual growth. Malkuth is the farthest point from Kether, the state where the forces originating in the Unmanifest take on the complex forms of the material world. Malkuth, therefore, represents not the lowest form of life, but the ultimate expression of God made Manifest.

'There is no part of me that is not of the gods.' This is true. The designs and interactions of the world are wonderful. There are no mythical creature's stranger than those life has designed (the platypus beats them all hands down!), nothing more perfect than the symmetry of a snowflake or more glorious than a sunset. Yet we look down on our own bodies with shame and disgust, conditioned by centuries of religious dogma and imposed morality, forgetting that they too are marvels of organic engineering. Where is the shame in being made in the image of God?

The only ugliness in the world can be laid squarely at the feet of Man.

Yesod provides the framework for the forms of Malkuth. It the point where everything is filtered, organised, and prepared for life as our limited perceptions see it. Yet although Malkuth sits apart from the Tree, it is still a part of it, intimately connected to each of the other spheres through Yesod.

The God Name is Adonai ha-Aretz, Lord of Earth, implying majesty, not the grubbiness we have been taught to associate with earthly things in a spiritual context. It is also called the Bride and the Kingdom. The Bride calls forth the creative forces of her Groom and the very existence of Malkuth, therefore, must call out to Kether. A King is not a king without a Kingdom and there would be no point in Kether without Malkuth.

Malkuth is the ultimate material expression of the forces which emanate from Kether. As we each carry that divine spark within use, it may be our task to learn all this phase of existence can teach us to return it to our Source to allow It, in turn, to grow.

The Spiritual Vision associated with Malkuth is the Knowledge and Conversation of the Holy Guardian Angel. This is the task of learning to know our true higher self, our true goals, and our true place in the grand scheme. At a basic level, we grow from childhood and begin to listen to our conscience as life teaches us the difference between right and wrong. In cosmic terms, we are all as children and have so very much to learn. The Holy Guardian Angel is that higher self which survives life and death and ultimately makes the return to the Light, enriched with experience, to add its mote to the Source of all life. It is a huge responsibility, and this world is the arena we have been given in which to complete this part of the task.

# Appendix 2

## *The Qabalistic Cross*

Readers may wish to begin each Exercise with a small ritual, to establish intent and provide an environment of Light in which to work. It does not matter what ritual you choose… a simple prayer, a globe of visualised Light, a protective Guardian… whatever feels right to you is the best opening for you!

The Qabalistic Cross is a classic ritual used by students of the Western Esoteric Tradition, a system largely based on the study of the Tree of Life. The ritual takes only a few moments but is invaluable for grounding the student in the moment, calling down divine Light and placing any operation under the Aegis of the Lords of Light.

It is useful to perform the ritual, but if you are not able to do so, it can be just as effective if you visualise the rite and vibrate the Names in silence.

Stand and face the east. Imagine a bright white sphere of Light, infinitely pure, above your head. A shaft of light streams down and passes through your body, following your gestures to form a cross that passes through you vertically from the heavens to earth and horizontally across the shoulders. This is not a uniquely Christian symbol, but the symbol of balanced force.

1.  Stand facing the East.

2. Extend the index and middle fingers, thumb and last two fingers folded into the palm. Touch the forehead and say "Eheieh" (Ay-hee-yay)

3. Touch the solar plexus and say "Malkuth" (Mal-koot)

4. Touch the left shoulder and say "ve Geburah" (vay gev-oo-rah)

5. Touch the right shoulder and say "ve Gedulah" (vey ged-oo-lah)

6. Clasp the fingers together, as in prayer, hold the hands to the centre of the chest, and say "le olahm amen" (lay ol-arm, amen)

The words mean, translated very basically,

> Eheieh -Thou art
> Malkuth - the Kingdom
> ve Geburah - the Power
> ve Gedulah - the Glory
> le olahm-unto the ages
> amen-so be it

This refers to the Sephirah or spheres of the Tree of Life.

Eheieh is the Divine Name associated with Kether, the highest sphere, the Point within the Circle, and means I Am.

Malkuth is the Kingdom, the tenth sphere, that of Earth, whose God Name is Adonai ha-Artez.

Geburah, the fifth sphere, is associated with Mars and is the destroyer of the effete, the great cleansing force of creation. The God Name is Elohim Gebor, The Almighty God.

Gedulah, also known as Chesed, is the fourth sephirah, the great law giver and merciful king, whose God name is El, God.

The hands clasped on the breast, touches Tiphareth, the centre of harmony of all things, whose Divine name is IHVH, (yod, hay, vav, hay, the four letters of the Tetragrammaton) Eloah va Daath, which loosely means God made manifest through mind.

Bear in mind that the moment you begin using ritual, the space where you work becomes a Temple of Light. Conduct yourself with all the reverence and respect that you would use in any other holy place. Be courteous to the presences and forces gathered there, for you will not stand alone, even though you may be unaware. Remember too that ritual *works*. It is a physical manifestation of action upon the Inner planes. Approach the rite with intent, perhaps take a purifying ritual bath with candles, herbs, incense... or just ritually wash your hands before you begin... intent matters more than anything else.

If you make a mistake, don't worry, just go back, and start that part again. Smile at yourself, you won't get blasted by demons! Joy, too, is allowed and any Divinity who could dream up the giraffe and the platypus *must* have a sense of humour!

# Appendix 3

## *The Elemental Triangles*

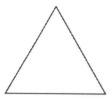 Fire

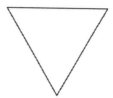 Water

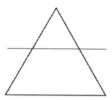 Air

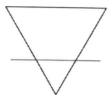 Earth

# About the Authors

## *G. Michael Vasey*

G. Michael Vasey is a Yorkshire man and rabid Tigers (Hull City AFC) fan that has spent most of his adult life lost deep in Texas and more lately, in the Czech Republic. While lucky enough to write for a living as a leading analyst in the commodity trading and risk management industry, he surreptitiously writes strange poems and equally strange books and stories on the topics of metaphysics, occult, and the paranormal on the side, hoping that one-day, someone might buy them.

After growing up experiencing ghosts, poltergeist, and other strange and scary experiences, he developed an interest in magic and the esoteric. These days he fancies himself as a bit of a mystic and a magician to boot. Most of his inspiration for his scribbling comes from either meditation or occasionally, very loud heavy metal music.

He blogs on substack, as well as at his own websites, vlogs on youtube, and hosts a podcast series called the magical world of G. Michael Vasey.

*Other books by G. Michael Vasey:*

- **Shadows & Strangeness: A Collection of True Ghost Stories, Hauntings and Weirdness** (*ebook and paperback*)
- **Whispers in the Darkness – A Story Sampler** (*ebook*)
- **Liminal People** (*ebook, paperback*)
- **Chasing the Goddess** (*ebook, paperback*)
- **A Questionable Science – Love and Death in the time of COVID (with Stuart France)** (*ebook, paperback*)
- **Chasing Dragons in Moravia** (*ebook, paperback*)
- **Chasing the Shaman** (*ebook, paperback*)
- **The Scary Best of My Haunted Life Too** (ebook, paperback)
- **Paranormal Eyewitness Compilation** (*ebook, paperback*)
- **Motel Hell** (ebook)
- **G. Michael Vasey's Halloween Vault of Horror** (*ebook*)
- **The Seduction of the Innocents** (*ebook, audiobook, and Paperback*)
- **The Chilling, True Terror of the Black-Eyed Kids – A Compilation** (*Paperback, Audiobook,and ebook*)
- **Poltergeist – The Noisy Ghosts** (*ebook*)
- **Ghosts of the Living** (*ebook*)
- **Your Haunted Lives 3 – The Black Eyed Kids** (*audiobook*)
- **Lord of the Elements (The Last Observer 2)** (*ebook and Paperback*)
- **True Tales of Haunted Places** (*ebook, audiobook*)
- **The Most Haunted Country in the World – The Czech Republic** (*ebook, paperback, audiobook. hardback*)
- **Your Haunted Lives – Revisited** (*ebook and Audiobook*)
- **The Pink Bus** (*ebook and audio book*)
- **Ghosts in The Machines** (*ebook and audiobook*)
- **The New You** (*Paperback, ebook and audiobook*)
- **God's Pretenders – Incredible Tales of Magic and Alchemy** (*ebook and audiobook*)

- **My Haunted Life – Extreme Edition** *(Paperback, audiobook and ebook)*
- **My Haunted Life 3** *(Audiobook and eBook)*
- **My Haunted Life Too** *(Audio book and ebook)*
- **My Haunted Life** *(ebook and audiobook)*
- **The Last Observer** *(Paperback, ebook and Audiobook)*
- **The Mystical Hexagram** *(Paperback and ebook)*
- **Inner Journeys – Explorations of the Soul** *(Paperback and ebook)*

## Poetry Collections

- **A Tribe of One** *(ebook)*
- **Slavic Tales** (ebook and paperback)
- **Reflections on Life: Spiritual Poetry** *(ebook and paperback)*
- **The Dilemma of Fatherhood** *(ebook)*
- **Death on The Beach** *(ebook)*
- **The Art of Science** *(Paperback, audiobook, ebook)*
- **Best Laid Plans and Other Strange Tails** *(Paperback and ebook)*
- **Moon Whispers** *(Paperback and ebook)*
- **Astral Messages** *(Paperback and ebook)*
- **Poems for the Little Room** *(Paperback and ebook)*
- **Weird Tales** *(Paperback and ebook)*

## Sue Vincent

**Sue Vincent** is a Yorkshire born writer and a Director of The Silent Eye. She has been immersed in the Mysteries all her life. Sue lives in Buckinghamshire, having been stranded there some years ago due to an accident with a blindfold, a pin, and a map. She nevertheless travels with co-author Stuart France, visiting the ancient sites of Albion, the hidden country of the heart. She is currently owned by a small dog who also blogs. **scvincent.com**

**The Silent Eye School of Consciousness** is a modern Mystery School that seeks to allow its students to find the inherent magic in living and being. With students around the world the school offers a fully supervised and practical correspondence course that explores the self through guided inner journeys and daily exercises. It also offers workshops that combine sacred drama, lectures, and informal gatherings to bring the teachings to life in a vivid and exciting format. The Silent Eye operates on a not-for-profit basis. Full details of the school may be found on the official website: www.thesilenteye.co.uk

***Other books by Sue Vincent:***

The Osiriad: Isis and Osiris, the Divine Lovers

Sword of Destiny, a magical novel

Notes from a Small Dog: Four Legs on Two

Laughter Lines

Life Lines

***With Stuart France:***

*Triad of Albion:*

The Initiate: Adventures in Sacred Chromatography

Heart of Albion: Tales from the Wondrous Head

Giants Dance: Rhyme and Reason

*The Doomsday Series:*

Doomsday: The Ætheling Thing

Doomsday: Dark Sage

Doomsday: Scions of Albion

*Lands of Exile*

But 'n' Ben

*Graphic Novels*

Mister Fox: The Legend

The Black Shade of Beeley

***Available in Paperback & for Kindle via Amazon worldwide***

Printed in Great Britain
by Amazon

29014032R00084